THE HISPANIC SOCIETY OF AMERICA

HISPANIC
NOTES & MONOGRAPHS

ESSAYS, STUDIES, AND BRIEF
BIOGRAPHIES ISSUED BY THE
HISPANIC SOCIETY OF AMERICA

PENINSULAR SERIES

Gregorio Fernandez ynsigne Escultor Natural del Reyno de Galicia, Becino de Valladolid en donde florecio con grandes creditos de su abeli dad y murio el año de 1636, a los 70, de su hedad en 22 de enero

GREGORIO FERNANDEZ

BY

BEATRICE I. GILMAN

Corresponding Member of The Hispanic
Society of America

THE HISPANIC SOCIETY
OF AMERICA
NEW YORK
1926

OXFORD UNIVERSITY PRESS
AMERICAN BRANCH
NEW YORK

PREFACE

This work can pretend to be no more than a preliminary compilation, from available sources, of material concerning Gregorio Fernández. An attempt has been made to present the sculptor's work in its proper setting and to treat it with some regard for the spirit in which it was created. Whatever its actual value as sculpture may be, a good share of its interest lies in its intimate connection with certain phases of Spanish life and thought.

CONTENTS

HISPANIC   NOTES

CONTENTS

AND MONOGRAPHS

PLATES

AND MONOGRAPHS

GREGORIO FERNANDEZ

INTRODUCTION

The beginning of the seventeenth cen- Founda-tions of seventeenth-century sculpture in Spain tury found European sculpture, under the guidance of Italy, on the threshold of the baroque. But while that movement in France was retarded by the continued influence of Giovanni da Bologna and classicism, in Spain it was preluded by a series of sculptors who were comparatively quiet and simple in their use of naturalistic methods, sincere and restrained while sharing the "perfervid Catholicism of the epoch". Gregorio Fernández (1) was the leader in a *détente* which drew Spanish sculpture away from the broad highway down a bypath largely free from foreign influences.

Spain in the previous centuries had shared the general ebb and flow of artistic movements throughout Europe, modifying them as her temperament demanded. During the Romanesque and Gothic periods the pilgrimage roads worked toward a uniformity of sculptural styles in the many countries which they traversed. The sixteenth century marked in Spain a more definite divergence from the main current. Although the Renaissance trained Spanish sculptors in its external forms, it could not inspire them with fervour for archæological research nor delight in beauty for beauty's sake. Its light, but faintly reflected from Italy, never shone in direct splendour. The superficial influence of Michael Angelo led to a fondness for muscular, agitated figures and twisted draperies, a proto-baroque movement reaching a first climax in the intense dramatism of Berruguete and a second in the violent contortions of Juní. Since the classicism to which the baroque was a reaction had never gained a hold upon Spain, it was natural that her sculpture should show a reaction in the opposite direction, away from the frenzy of motion, the exaggerated individualism of the late six-

teenth century, to a period of greater calm
and simplicity. Certain minor characteristics of the contemporary Italian style
found a harmonious place in the Spanish
scheme. Pictorial adjuncts, by no means
an innovation, were received with enthu-
siasm, nor was the lack of feeling for the
medium a new phenomenon. Spanish art,
more exclusively than that of any other
country, had been dominated by the
peculiarly national brand of sombre, im-
passioned Catholicism. The change of
manner involved no break in the underlying forces which shaped her sculpture.
Since the aristocracy had never, as in other
countries, monopolized art for its own
aggrandizement, the emotional, literal faith
of the people continued to demand satisfaction in lifelike and dramatic representations of religious subjects. It was this
compulsion which led to the continued use
of wood, so warmly espoused by the Flemish in Gothic days, and of polychromy.
"For a Spanish Catholic," says Señora
Pardo Bazán (2), "a statue of marble or

alabaster would always be cold: we need
to humanize the divine image, give it
colours, clothes, and flesh tints, see the
blood of the wounds, the livid flesh; the
rosy little body of the Child Jesus moves
us; and the pallor of the ascetic, his un-
kempt beard, his eyes glassy with unshed
tears, and his bare feet, soiled by the dust
of the road, edify us."

I

Although Gregorio Fernández's prestige
has been limited to his native land, he is
the initiator and an outstanding figure of
a movement in Spanish sculpture which
occupied the better part of the seventeenth
century. Since the old order but grudg-
ingly gives place to the new, certain elements in Fernández's work can be traced
to his predecessors. Valladolid, the city in
which he lived, was rich in their work, and
their progress in technique not to be ig-
nored. Berruguete had dwelt opposite the
Monastery of *San Benito* in which was
housed his great *retablo* (now in the *Museo
Provincial*). In the city likewise had lived
Gaspar Becerra, although the only undis-
puted work of his now there is the skeleton
figure in the *Museo Provincial*. Juan de
Juní, whose house Fernández was later to
inhabit, carved, among other things, *The
Entombment* (also in the *Museo Provin-*

cial) for the Convent of *San Francisco* and the celebrated *Our Lady of the Swords* in the Church of *las Angustias*. To him, in particular, his successor owed much. Juní had modified the Renaissance mannerisms and adapted them to suit his very individual temperament, but he was more closely linked with the period just past than with the one about to begin. Certain types of faces and some peculiarities in the treatment of draperies which Fernández affected were derived from him. Near Juní was established Esteban Jordán, of a quieter artistic temperament, whose work may be seen in the *retablo* of the Church of *la Magdalena*. The simplified architectural scheme of Fernández's *retablos* may be the outcome of Jordán's influence, since his school was preponderant in Valladolid during the early years of the seventeenth century. Francisco Giralte is represented in the same church by the *retablo* of the Chapel of *los Corrales*. Of these men Esteban Jordán alone lingered until the last years of the sixteenth century.

In Fernández's own time there was a dearth of good artists in Valladolid. They seem to have been men of much smaller calibre whose names are known only in connection with minor works. Pompeo Leoni, summoned from Italy by Philip the Second to assist in adorning the grim immensity of the Escorial, was a transient visitor in Valladolid. He left an abiding record of his presence in the bronze statues of the Duke and Duchess of Lerma. With these monuments is also linked the name of Juan de Arfe, most famed for his custodias, miniature temples of silver and gold.

Although native painters were few and of little merit, there was an abundance of men of letters. It was in his unsavoury quarters in the *Rastro* that Cervantes dwelt when he obtained (in 1604) the royal privilege to publish the first part of the adventures of that " Ingenious Knight, Don Quixote de la Mancha ". Góngora, although in his sonnets he abuses the city, came here in an unfruitful search for royal preferment, as did also his fellow-stylists,

Contempo-
raries

the ill-starred Count of Villamediana and
the poet-priest Paravicino. The mention
of these few names is an indication of that
interest in art and literature which gave the
seventeenth century the proud title of
Spain's "Golden Age".

Even in the simple court of Philip the
Second artists and men of letters had received their due. His mild successor,
unbridled by the frugal tastes of his father,
included the arts among those luxuries on
which he squandered the revenues of his
kingdom while famine and misery infested
the towns and countryside. Wars in the
Low Countries and wars in Italy failed to
disturb the ease-loving monarch, who left
such cares to his ministers while he only
complained that his subjects did not provide him with sufficient means to uphold
his royal state. Elaborate court festivals,
hunting expeditions, bullfights, and *juegos
de cañas* were the order of the day, and
the favourite, the Duke of Lerma, and
other satellites vied with each other in
providing entertainment for a king who

Philip the
Third

PLATE I

RETABLO MAYOR
Attributed in part to Fernández
Valladolid. Church of San Miguel

was so liberal in bestowing offices, estates, and incomes on those who found favour in his eyes. With all his love of sport and of luxury, this was no king who placed his entire faith in earthly pleasures. True to the tradition of a line of sovereigns who had shown themselves the champions of Catholicism in Europe, Philip the Third spent three hours a day at his devotions and begrudged no expenditure which was devoted to the erection and adornment of churches and religious houses. His Queen, Margaret of Austria, was no whit behind him in pious deeds. What the rulers did the court followed. Nobles anxious to win royal preferment sought to increase their credit on this earth as well as the next by lavish gifts to religious institutions. Thus it came about that the faculties of the architect, the painter, the sculptor, and the silversmith were called into use for the building of chapels, the composition of *retablos*, the carving of mortuary statues and monuments, and the elaboration of church plate.

Valladolid
at the
beginning
of the seven-
teenth
century

Valladolid was especially favoured in the endowment of churches and convents since it was the seat of the Court from 1601 to 1606 and was also one of the residences of the Duke of Lerma and his unfortunate protégé, Rodrigo Calderón. It was largely through the influence of the Duke that Philip was persuaded to restore to the city its ancient glory as the seat of power, although the pressure of the other nobles and the distressful pleas of Madrid very shortly compelled the King to move the Court there again. Thus the city, stirred to sudden life by the advent of royalty, lapsed into a state of torpor from which it was aroused only by the continued solicitude of the Duke of Lerma, and by occasional royal visits and festivals. Fernández seems to have profited only from the general stimulation of interest in art. The few specific instances in which he benefited from court patronage were his commission for temporary decorations in the palace, the *Cristo del Pardo*, and a *Saint Anne*. The contracts for his other work were made with the chapters of churches or with their founders. He seems never to have been dependent upon the fickle interest of royal patrons, although the restrictions laid upon him by church authorities were fairly onerous.

It is hard to conceive of the Valladolid of to-day, a city of monotonous level streets with buildings the hue of the all-pervading dust, as the birthplace of kings and the scene of many a stirring drama. The flamboyant façades of *San Gregorio* and *San Pablo* and the austere mansions where was once the royal abode, crumbling relics of a past era, arouse scarce a flicker of romantic interest. The streets are not exempt from the evil odours and noises of other Spanish cities, nor have they the variety and mellowness of age which give to Toledo and to Burgos their peculiar charm. There is nothing to palliate the overpowering, fierce light which the sun pours into the open spaces. One with the uninteresting plain over which it spreads, no individual mark distinguishes the town.

Although the Spanish accounts of Valladolid in the time of Fernández are replete with adulation, the reports of foreigners are not unmixed praise. Joly, writing in 1603–1604, complains of the dirtiness and muddiness of the streets, while Enrique Cock (3), in 1592, deals out approbation and censure with a judicious hand:

"The *plaça mayor* is large and square, and all its buildings of one style, as also the *platería* and the other neighbouring streets, which, since a large part of the city was burned in the year 68 [actually 1561], were ordered built with symmetry and unity, the city helping to this effect those who built. . . In addition Valladolid has for its recreation the *prado* or *campo de la Madalena,* where there are good drives and shady walks by which to cross the Esgueva, and here every night in the summer foregather many people to enjoy themselves and take the air, bringing their supper there for their pleasure, and horsemen go there to exercise their horses;

PLATE II

SAINT FRANCIS XAVIER
Valladolid. Church of San Miguel

and since the sovereigns of Castilla used to make it their custom to repair hither, there are throughout the city many houses of titled noblemen and grandees. . . The egresses of this city are on level ground without elevations or depressions, since it is situated in a plain, and the best ones are on the banks of the river, where there are gardens and pleasure houses for recreation. The only thing lacking in this town is good water, since there is no fountain within it, and the people drink from the Pisuerga, nor clocks to know, hear, and see the time of day; and it has an abundance of rogues, wenches, disputes, dust, stones, hogs, dogs, vermin, and fleas, and all during the winter continual fogs so that day is almost like night for days at a time. . . The people, although half-way courteous, are proud and very presumptuous, to the extent that it is said and almost all hold it true that Valladolid is the best place in Christendom. I know not whether they err by reason of the popular refrain which they quote, *Villa por villa, Valladolid en Castilla,* or if they err from their lack of experience in not having seen other lands or from being ignorant and presumptuous fools, because their fancy is that Valladolid is better than Flanders, Naples, and Rome, while actually Valladolid is, so to speak, a barnyard compared with the principal cities of Flanders, Naples, Rome, Venice, and others."

With these physical characteristics there must be borne in mind the fact that Valladolid was a centre of religious feeling. Not only was it the seat of the Inquisition up to the advent of the Court, but it had been the scene of a drastic suppression of heresy in several autos-da-fé during the sixteenth century. Even in Fernández's time two minor ones were held.

It was in such a city, of no great charm in itself, but with the tradition of a long line of sculptors of importance, a tradition which he was to carry on in his own way, that Fernández spent the greater portion of his life.

II

The first recorded contract in which Fernández is mentioned is from Valladolid. In the year 1605 he was associated with Milan Vilmercati (Vimercado, as the Spaniards called him), a Milanese who came to Spain in the company of Pompeo Leoni, in the construction of a little temple for the festivities attendant upon the birth of Philip the Fourth of Spain. This temple, the architectural portion of which was due to Cristóbal Velázquez, was erected in the salon of the house of the Count of Miranda, then annexed to the royal palace, and was adorned with nine decorative statues in whose composition Fernández assisted. For this work he received a total of four hundred and seventy *reales*. Pinheiro da Veiga (4), in his contemporary narrative, describes the structure as follows: " At the head of the room, instead of a canopy was made a throne, in the form of a triumphal arch; twelve strong, fluted columns form it with its portico and façade, the latter representing the temple of Virtue with Fame on the dome, and on the capitals, life-size figures of angels. . ." In this year the sculptor's name appears as the head of a family in the books of the parish of *San Ildefonso*.

Birth

The incidents of his life previous to this date are largely a matter of conjecture. According to tradition he was born in Galicia. Ceán Bermúdez (5), without stating his authorities, suggests Pontevedra as the actual spot. Martí y Monsó (6), finding record of a bequest to the church of the little town of Sarria, Galicia, made by him at his death and mentioned by his widow in her testament, thought that this interest in a village so far from his usual residence might indicate some connection with the place in his earlier years. Martí's investigations were fruitless, nor is there any documentary evidence to throw light

PLATE III

SAINT IGNATIUS OF LOYOLA
Valladolid. Church of San Miguel

on the problem. The date, likewise, is uncertain, early writers placing it at 1566. Much confusion was caused by the inscription on his portrait which, reading originally that he " died the year 1622 at 70 years of age ", was partially changed in accordance with later discoveries to read " died the year 1636 at 70 years of age " (7). In a lawsuit (8) dated 1610 in which he appears as an appraiser, he states that he is thirty-four years old. Although this is not necessarily an exact statement, it fixes his birth approximately at the year 1576.

Mystery also surrounds the reason for his appearance in Valladolid. Sometime before 1605 he had married María Pérez, whose parents, natives of Madrid and of Nava del Carnero, as is stated in her will, owned a house in the *Calle de la Paloma,* Madrid. Since no record of Fernández's marriage has been found in Valladolid, it may be presumed that this event occurred in Madrid. A plausible hypothesis is that he was among the band of artists and

Marriage

craftsmen who followed the Court when it moved to Valladolid, although the commission for decorative figures and the notices concerning the *Cristo del Pardo* and *Saint Anne* are the only existing records which connect him with the royal house. Of the length of his stay in Madrid, if, indeed, he stayed there at all, of his life before that time, we have no knowledge. If the sculptor came to Valladolid as part of the following of the Court, why did he choose to remain in this city when it sank into stagnation at the removal of the royal residence? It was then no longer the centre of artistic activity which it had formerly been. Even the few artists who still continued to work there were not of his own stature. Whatever reasons he may have had, there he fixed his abode, not to change it during his lifetime. He may have had to make some journeys in connection with his work, but the usual procedure seems to have been to carve them in his own studio and then ship them to their destination.

Of his relatives notice is given only of a brother, Juan Alvarez, whose relationship is proved by the notice of his death: "'On the eighth of March of this year (1630) died Juan Alvarez sculptor brother of Gregorio Fernandez . . .'" (9). Of Fernández's two children, the son, Gregorio, born in 1605, lived only until 1610. The daughter, Damiana, born in 1607, was married four times before she reached the age of thirty. Her first husband was Miguel de Elizalde, a sculptor employed in her father's studio. The contract was signed on the sixteenth of July, 1621, and it was stipulated in it that the son-in-law was to continue in Fernández's employ for at least two years at the same salary which he was then receiving. His death in the following year prevented the fulfillment of his contract. Sometime before 1624 the young widow took for her second husband Juan Pérez de Lanciego, a doctor, since at that date their names appear as *padrinos* at a wedding. Of this union was born a daughter, Teresa, and a posthumous son.

After the death of the doctor, Damiana
turned again to her father's profession for
a spouse, marrying (February 7th, 1633)
Juan Francisco de Hibarne, a sculptor,
native of Zaragoza, who, not much more
fortunate than his predecessors, died in
1635. Damiana's last marriage, to Juan
Rodríguez Gavilán, linen merchant, which
took place September 21st, 1636, was of
greater duration. They had eight children,
of whom seven reached maturity. It appears then, due to her marital vicissitudes,
that Damiana must have been a member
of her father's household most of the time
during his life.

House

In the year 1615 Fernández moved from
the *Calle del Sacramento,* purchasing a
dwelling nearby " ' . . . outside the *puerta
del Campo* . . . in the *hacera del mones-
terio de santi-spiritus* facing the monastery
of *nr̄a señora del carmen* and on the corner of the *calle de san luis* . . .' " (10).
This house had already acquired fame because of its previous owner, Juan de Juní.
In the time of Charles the Fifth, Alonso

PLATE IV

RETABLO MAYOR
Vitoria. Church of San Miguel

Niño de Castro, in view of his loyalty
during the war of the *Comunidades,* had
been granted a tract of land outside the
Puerta del Campo. Four lots of this he
sold to Juní, who later purchased two
more. Here the sculptor built his house.
After his death it passed through the hands
of various members of his family and, for
a short time, into those of a stranger,
Simón Méndez, the Portuguese, with whom
Cervantes had some dealings. There are
indications that during Méndez's régime
Pompeo Leoni may have lodged in this
dwelling. A daughter of his was living in
it at the time of her marriage, when Leoni
is known to have been in Valladolid. It
was from Ana María de Juní, grand-
daughter of the famous sculptor, that
Fernández purchased the residence. The
neighbourhood must have been pleasant, a
favourite recreation spot, described by
Pinheiro da Veiga (11) in the following
terms:

". . . the *Puerta del Campo* . . . is at
the entrance of the city, and . . . has in

front of it a square or *rocío* . . . encompassed about by houses, many of them very illustrious, where for the most part dwell ambassadors, and so spacious that it has around it nine monasteries and hospitals, in addition to the fact that it is very beautiful, very level, and so large that the colours of the people's clothes cannot be distinguished, and a battle could be given in it, and in winter it is the promenade of the Court, where they go to take the sun in a place which overlooks the river with very beautiful views, which they call the *Espolón*. . .

"Afterward the road continues to Simancas, between the *Carmen* and *Sancti-Spíritus*, the river remaining on the right-hand with many villas and woodlands, and at the left very level plains as far as eye can see."

The *Campo Grande* remains to the present day, but the *Acera de Sancti Spíritus* has changed its name to the *Paseo de Zorrilla*, and the house, according to Martí (12), is forty-two of the present numbering. Bosarte (13) described its condition at the beginning of the nineteenth century as follows:

" The door is an arch of good stone, and the wall begins to rise with several courses of squared stones; the rest is masonry or brick and mud walls. The wooden doors are very old, with thick nails without any design whatever, and may be the original ones of Juní. One enters by the only door of the house into a patio, now unpaved, in which there are no traces of there ever having been arches, or posts, or columns. . . On the left-hand is visible on the same floor and on a level with the patio the room which was the studio of the sculptor. Since the house forms the corner of the little street of *San Luis,* and its entrance is on the *Campo grande,* part of the windows of the studio open on the *calle de San Luis,* and part on the *Campo grande.* The windows give no sign of ever having had gratings or iron balconies. . ."

The dealings with the Juní family concerning this property are a clue to an in-

Friends

timacy which must have been firm and lasting between the two families. Time and again they acted as *padrinos* at weddings and births in each other's households. In addition, Juan de Muniátegui, Ana María de Jíní's first husband, is recorded as *fiador* for Fernández in the contract for the sculpture of the *retablo* of the Church of *San Miguel,* and Ana María, at her death, named the latter as her executor. Since these mutual relations do not appear on record before the year 1606, it may be a slight indication that Fernández's stay in Valladolid did not date from a much earlier period.

With the sculptor, Manuel del Rincón, Fernández seems likewise to have had friendly intercourse, since Rincón was a witness at Damiana's first wedding (1621), and Fernández a *padrino* at that of Rincón himself. If Fray Matías de Sobremonte (14), the historian of the Convent of *San Francisco,* is to be believed, this relationship dates to the time of Manuel's father, Francisco, who was "teacher of the

PLATE V

MATER DOLOROSA
Valladolid. Church of la Cruz

great Gregorio Fernández at the beginning of his career." Since Francisco del Rincón was still living in 1606, this does not disturb the hypothesis that Fernández may have come to Valladolid in the train of Philip the Third and have worked under this master for a few years before his first known commission, that in conjunction with Vilmercati. His supposed teacher was the man who carved the stone figures for the façade of *Nuestra Señora de las Angustias* and also some figures for the *pasos* of the Church of *la Pasión*.

Fernández's last years must have been Ill health a period of continual suffering, for in a letter written in 1629 by the representative of the Chapter of Plasencia Cathedral, then resident in Valladolid, concerning the *retablo* on which the sculptor was working, this official writes that the artist " ' . . . is always in such poor health and has been dangerously ill so many times, and sometimes despaired of even before he undertook the work, and after having undertaken it, this has been the most dangerous of his illnesses . . .'" (15). Again, concerning the *retablo* of the church at Aránzazu, it is written, "'I, fearing that the aforesaid Gregorio might die before finishing the aforesaid *retablos,* in order to place him under greater obligations, in the month of February, 1635, gave him 500 *ducados* . . .'" (16). That these fears were not without foundation was proved in the following year, for on the twenty-second of January, 1636, Gregorio Fernández died and was buried in his tomb in the Monastery of the *Carmen Calzado,* leaving provision that a hundred masses be said for his soul. For a long time it was supposed that he died in 1622, following the inscription on his tomb, but that error was corrected by the discovery of the parish record which disclosed the fact that the date on his tomb referred only to the year in which it was acquired.

The letter from the official of Plasencia Cathedral, previously cited, gives some insight into the personality of Fernández. After complaining that some of the canons

Death

Personality

PLATE VI

MATER DOLOROSA

Valladolid. Museo Provincial de Bellas Artes

had annoyed the sculptor by writing him
letters of reproof for his apparent delay,
the author says:

" 'You see, then . . . what effect it may
have to write offensive remarks to a man
who, aside from being an honourable
gentleman, is of a very sensitive and
irascible temperament; it being true for
the most part, that after he has some
health to be able to work, he has done it
with much care, and a great desire to
finish, and give satisfaction in everything,
as will be seen clearly in the report of
what has been done . . .' " (17).

This apparent irritability may have been
due to the state of his health, since other
notices seem to point to great generosity
and kindness of disposition: for a sculptor
employed in his studio who died in ex-
treme poverty he ordered eight masses;
a servant who died in his house was buried
at his expense in one of the best sepulchres
in the church; a foundling left at his door
was cared for and, at death, given Chris-
tian burial. It is stated that his brother

had only such goods as Fernández gave him. Poverty seems to have been the proper condition of a sculptor in those days, since many a notice of death relates that the person made no will because he had nothing of which to dispose. The probity of Fernández's character is attested by the frequency with which he served as executor of wills. Two of his sons-in-law named him for this charge, while the Countess of Triviana, at her death, appointed him one of the appraisers of her possessions. He served twice as *mayordomo de fábrica* of his parish, supplying from his own pocket the deficit incurred during his second incumbency.

The fame of his art among his contemporaries is even better substantiated. The licentiate Cabeza Leal of the Chapter of Plasencia Cathedral speaks of him as "'the best artificer now known in the realm'" and says that "' . . . not only judges, but the lords and grandees of Spain, who have dealings with him and are present in the city, go to his house and like to see him work, honour him, and keep him cheerful and content, in order that he may carry on his work willingly . . .'" (18). In a document concerning a chapel endowed by Fray Juan de Orbea in the Monastery of the *Carmen Calzado* mention is made of a statue then in the hands of Gregorio Fernández, "'who is the best expert known in these times'" (19). A series of letters between this same man and Juan López de Issasi about the *retablo* for the Franciscan convent of Eibar abounds also in encomiums of the sculptor. López de Issasi writes that he has had a certain Ayala draw plans, "'I having stipulated that the image of the *Immaculate Conception* had to be of the excellence of *Gregorio Hernandez,* since it seemed to me that a man so sought after and so modest would not wish to take upon himself the entire *retablo*. . . Also it seemed to me that for a man of such excellence the sum of 3000 *ducados* was small . . .'" (20). To all this, Fray Juan, urging the engagement of Fernández for the whole work, replies, " ' What is certain is that I wish this work to be noteworthy, and it will be to such a degree that when this man is dead, there will not be money enough in this world with which to pay what he has done . . .' " (21). After his death his relatives are distinguished by their connection with " ' the late Gregorio Fernández, the noted sculptor ' " (22), and the Duchess of Alburquerque, purchasing a statue from his widow, especially stipulated that it be by his hand and not by one of his employees.

Nor was he at all oblivious to the value of his own work, since a letter concerning the *retablo* of the church of Aránzazu says that he " ' . . . made the declaration of the aforesaid *retablos* with great reluctance, because he wished them to be evaluated, for the greater gain which would ensue to him . . .' " (23). His comparative freedom from lawsuits, however, implies that his demands were not immoderate.

One cannot evolve a personality from notices like these, but the brief facts about his life show him as a man of humble family and circumstances leading a quiet, laborious existence, enlivened only by intercourse with his friends. Since the statements concerning his ill health indicate that at least during the last decade of his life he was a semi-invalid, he must be counted among those indomitable spirits whose work has been achieved despite infirmities of the body. There are no indications that he was a man of education. Without contact with foreign lands, removed at an early period from the atmosphere of the court, he must have shared to a remarkable extent the tastes and sentiments of the common people among whom he lived. His art could not fail to reflect these influences. It was their longing for vivid pictures, their simplicity and intensity of emotion which he must satisfy by life-like and moving images of Saviour and saints.

III

Gregorio Fernández's work, done entirely in wood, is limited to *retablos*, both elaborate compositions for high altars and single figures or groups of figures for less important posts, and to processional images. The *retablo*, that towering structure which might combine architecture and painting, architecture and sculpture, or all three, had at this period reached a stage of development analogous to the Greco-Roman style of architecture sponsored by Herrera.

In the plateresque products of the sixteenth century such masters as Berruguete and Giralte had conceived the *retablo* as an entity in which the architectural framework, enriched with multitudinous carvings on column and entablature, together with the actual statues and scenes set in the frame were part and parcel of one conception. In those days the master sculptor not only drew the design for the *retablo* but was personally responsible for the entire work of executing and erecting it, perhaps taking a hand in the carving of ornamental details as well as sculpturing the figures and scenes. The architecture of these *retablos,* consisting of columns, bases, and entablatures on a scale commensurate with the comparatively small size of the many reliefs and statues which composed the ensemble, was incidental to the carving which was lavished upon every inch of available space.

The latter part of the sixteenth century marked a certain degree of simplification and a gradual separation of the two elements, architecture and sculpture, to give the former more prominence. This movement is exemplified in the work of Esteban Jordán. The plan was bolder, with fewer and larger divisions, which entailed the use of larger architectural features, figures, and sculptured scenes or paintings. The ornamental carving was restricted to the lower part of the shafts of columns, to capitals, and to narrow friezes. Herrera reduced the *retablo* to stark simplicity in the one designed for the church of the Escorial.

The plan used by Fernández in his authentic *retablos* has only such variations as the space in which it was to be placed demanded. It betrays a basic similarity, in spite of its greater ornateness, to that originated by Herrera.

This plan, as illustrated in the documented *retablos* of the Church of *San Miguel,* Vitoria, the Franciscan convent at Eibar, and Plasencia Cathedral, usually consists of two stories and an attic. The structure rises from a broad base. The stories are separated by entablatures with narrow friezes supported by six fluted Corinthian columns spaced to provide panels of varying widths. The central panels are widest for the accommodation of the main compositions, the outer ones wide enough for reliefs, and those between narrow, to serve as niches for statues.

PLATE VIII

PIETA

Valladolid. Church of San Martin

The columns are placed on high pedestals which, in addition to bases below the panels, provide space for small reliefs or paintings of the cardinal virtues, the evangelists, or incidents from the Passion of Christ. The attic consists of four columns over the central panel surmounted by a broken pediment. The space thus enclosed is invariably devoted to the Crucifixion, accompanied by the Virgin and Saint John, set under a round arch and surmounted by the bust of God the Father in the tympanum of the pediment. Figures of saints fill the niches at the sides, and statues of angels above the end columns of the lower stories complete the structure. Above the central panel of the second story a broken pediment on which may sport two amorini frames a panel bearing the Dove of the Holy Spirit. A tabernacle is frequently the central feature of the first story. The niches for statues of the saints are finished with round arches, and garlands are swung between the capitals of the enclosing columns.

It is difficult to ascertain the exact degree of responsibility which Fernández bore in the construction of his *retablos*. The framework was entrusted, occasionally by a separate contract, as in the instance of the Church of *San Miguel*, Valladolid, to an official who bore the title of *ensamblador*. It is not entirely clear whether the master sculptor or the *ensamblador* was responsible for the architectural design. In the case of the *retablo* of the Church of *San Miguel*, Valladolid, the specifications and design were already drawn up before bids for the carpentry were received, but the contract for the sculpture was not signed until after that for the *ensamblaje*. This may mean that Fernández had already submitted his plan, but that the chapter would not draw up his contract until an *ensamblador* had been found. It is stated in Llaguno (24) that Diego de Basoco drew the plans for the *retablo* at Aránzazu. As for the ones still extant from which conclusions might be drawn, those of the Church of *San Miguel*,

PLATE IX

PIETA
Attributed to Fernández
Burgos.   Convent of the Carmen Descalzo

Vitoria, the Franciscan convent, Eibar, and Plasencia Cathedral are very similar in design. The architecture of the first was by an *ensamblador* named Velázquez, possibly Juan, but there is no statement as to whether sculptor or *ensamblador* drew the plan. That of the second, according to Ceán Bermúdez's additions to Llaguno (25), was by Juan de Maseras, who drew the plan. Francisco and Juan Velázquez are mentioned as *ensambladores* of the Plasencia *retablo*. If these notices are reliable, there is some possibility that the resemblance between the *retablos* of Vitoria and Plasencia might be due to the intervention of the same *ensamblador*, but there is no evidence that a Velázquez worked on the third. One may venture the hypothesis that the ideas embodied in these *retablos* were Fernández's, whereas the exact drawings were done by the *ensamblador* in accordance with the sculptor's desires. Whatever Fernández's ultimate responsibility, he seems to have been personally concerned only with the carving

of the statues and reliefs set in the niches
and panels. The ornamental details were
done by workmen called *entalladores*.

The sculpture is carried out in the same
monumental vein as its setting. Life-size
figures with dignified attitudes and massive
draperies fill the niches. The huge panels
are occupied by dramatis personæ in high
relief against a background in low relief,
either architectural or scenic, with great
consideration for the interpretation of the
incident but with little thought for sub-
tleties of composition. Fewer figures and
simpler backgrounds supplant the elaborate
detail of Gothic and Renaissance reliefs.
Tumultuous effects of light and shade re-
sult from the high relief and the deep
folds of the garments. Rocks and trees
are rendered by the crude conventions
which had survived since the Flemish trip-
tychs of the fifteenth century, although
they are simplified to accord with the larger
scale. Occasional whorls of clouds presage
the lavish use of sculptured clouds and
rays of light in later years. Masses in

which angles rather than curves predomi-
nate are substituted for the flowing lines of
composition and drapery which had been
introduced with the Renaissance by Berruguete and Forment. The draperies are
occasionally agitated, and the poses of the
figures, though simple, are dramatic. The
violent contortions and exaggerated pos-
tures in Juní's and Giralte's work are
abandoned for simpler conceptions em-
bodying a serener spirit. Throughout
Fernández's work there is no element of
struggle. The emphasis is upon the en-
durance of suffering; the relaxation rather
than the torture of death; and upon the
concentration rather than the transports
of religious ecstasy.

The treatment of folds is an important
element in defining the general character
of Fernández's sculpture. Abandoning the
exuberance of clinging, twisted draperies
which the Renaissance had affected, the
Valladolid sculptor returned to an earlier
tradition. His close affiliation with Gothic
principles in the matter of broad surfaces

and angular folds, sharply broken, is remarkable, but it seems more probable that
he derived his ideas from a direct obser-
vation of the stiff folds of costumes of
his own time. His bishops are encased
in copes as unyielding as those encrusted
with embroidery which weighed down
similar ecclesiastics in real life; his monks
and nuns still do penance in the harsh
woolens which were a part of their earthly
mortifications of the flesh. Without the
freedom and grace of diaphanous or clinging fabrics, these uncompromising garments
have a stern dignity in keeping with the
characters they clothe. Occasional short
transverse folds like indentations break the
long lines of cope and habit. At its best
the style is characterized by a laudable
breadth and simplicity; at its worst it is
rigid and uncouth. It ranges from the
severity of Saint Theresa's cape to the
fantastic, fluttering robes of the angels
poised atop the *retablo* of Plasencia
Cathedral.

The faces of his personages, less dis-

PLATE X

CHRIST AT THE COLUMN
Valladolid.   Church of la Cruz

torted by emotion than those of his predecessors, are modeled with clearer outlines and more sharply defined planes.
The features are more regular, with less
exaggerated characteristics and more re-
posed expressions. The Virgin's head is
usually of a monumental type, the Christ's
face thin and delicate. In the treatment
of the hair the sculptor has resorted to
thick, separate strands in regular undula-
tion.

In his figures of Christ, the only place
in which the nude appears, there is a
suavity of modeling far removed from
the muscular creations for whose vogue
Michael Angelo was responsible. The
forms are more elegant, less salient and
powerful. In the attitudes of his statues,
also, while not approaching the sweetness
of southern schools, he has affected an
elegance of bearing in which are the roots
of some of his mannerisms. In the standing figures the weight rests on one foot, a
posture which has been synonymous with
grace since the days of Polyclitus. A

slight inclination of the head emphasizes this effect. The hands are poised in dainty gestures inappropriate to the suffering Deity and ecstatic saints.

Fernández's sculptural style appears fully formed, even as his known history begins when he is already beyond his youth, nor is it possible to trace in it any development. This peculiarity is due to the uniform style of the few dated works. Since in the large *retablos* he often repeats figures, the same type may appear at opposite poles of his career. Due to these conditions it seems necessary to treat his work as an entity without any attempt at division into periods. It must also be borne in mind that he employed assistants in his studio who certainly helped in the execution of large *retablos,* and to whom Fernández may also have entrusted the carving of smaller works after he had drawn the design. This consideration makes it difficult to separate absolutely his personal work from that of his school.

Gregorio Fernández's initial appearance

in the archives of Valladolid, at the time of the birth of Philip the Fourth, has already been recorded. The following year witnessed his first important contract — that for the sculpture of the Church of *San Miguel*, which, although of ancient origin, had undergone various reforms and was now to receive a new *retablo* for its high altar. The contract (dated October 26th, 1606) gave minute specifications for the work. It called for nine large figures — Saints Peter, Paul, Philip, and James the Great, the Archangels Raphael and Gabriel, and the three characters of the Crucifixion, Christ on the Cross, the Virgin, and Saint John — and nine small figures — the four doctors of the church and five others, whose identity is not specified. For this work the sculptor received in all 4,280 *reales*. The statue of the titular saint was contracted for separately, commanding the sum of 604 *reales*. It was painted by Francisco Martínez and Pedro Salazar for 610 *reales*. The architectural framework was entrusted to Cristóbal

Retablo of the Church of *San Miguel*, Valladolid

Velázquez, the man who designed the decorative temple on which the sculpture by Vilmercati and Fernández had been placed. Velázquez was assisted by his son, Francisco, and by Diego de Basoco.

This original Church of *San Miguel* was torn down in 1777 and the parish, together with that of *San Julián,* was transferred to the Church of *San Ignacio,* left vacant by the suppression of the Company of Jesus. The authorship of the *retablo* of the present church (Plate I) is still a matter of conjecture. Although its architectural style is similar to that adopted by Fernández, there is considerable difference in detail. That of *San Miguel* varies from authentic ones in the use of columns of different orders in the various stories; in the introduction of two coats of arms flanking the architectural portion of the attic, in which statues of the four evangelists likewise figure; in the small panels containing paintings which fill the upper part of the spaces between the outer columns; and in the fact that the narrowest spaces are

PLATE XI

CRISTO DE LA LUZ

Valladolid. Museo Provincial de Bellas Artes

on the outside instead of between the central subjects and the other reliefs. In addition the entablatures, instead of being broken and set back to the level of the frames of the large panels, continue in an unbroken line flush with the outer faces of the capitals. In the central panel of the second story is a statue of Saint Michael and at the left and right the Resurrection and Pentecost in high reliefs. Below these appear, respectively, the tabernacle surmounted by figures of Saints Julian and Basilissa, the Adoration of the Shepherds, and the Circumcision. The outer niches contain statues of Saint Peter, Saint Paul, Saint James the Great, and Saint Philip. On the bases and pedestals of the second story are paintings, but on those of the lower, reliefs of the Cardinal Virtues and representations of the fathers of the Latin Church. Beside the steps of the presbytery, on pedestals, stand figures of the Archangels Raphael and Gabriel.

Concerning these components it is stated in a diary written by Ventura Pérez (26) that the *Saint Michael* was brought from the old Church of *San Miguel* and placed where *Saint Ignatius* had formerly stood. The statues of Saints Julian and Basilissa were brought from the old Church of *San Julián*. Thus the *Saint Michael* would seem to be the work of Gregorio Fernández, since he is known to have carved the image of the titular saint for the first church.

An attempt has been made (27) to identify nine of the statues of the present *retablo*, that is, the Crucifix, Virgin, and Saint John, the four saints in the side niches, and the two archangels standing by the presbytery steps, with the nine large figures of the contract. Although a coincidence in the subject matter and in the size has been discovered, the only ones which approximate Fernández's style are those of the apostles in the side niches. The Saint Paul is in much the same attitude as his counterpart in the *retablo* of Plasencia Cathedral. Of the other sculpture neither the reliefs of the main stories nor the evangelists of the upper stage show any affiliation with Fernández's style, but the reliefs of Virtues on the base are closely allied to those in the *retablo* of *San Miguel,* Vitoria.

The frame presents an even more difficult problem. Its general character is similar to that employed by Fernández, but it is improbable that the frame was transferred from the old Church of *San Miguel.* There are no records concerning the *retablo* of the new Church of *San Miguel* while it was under the tutelage of Saint Ignatius, but since the sculpture of the side altars appears to be by Fernández, and since work was being done on the church in the early years of the seventeenth century, there is ground for supposing that Fernández may have had a hand in the composition of the original *retablo mayor.*

The central figures on the side altars represent Saint Francis Xavier (Plate II) and Saint Ignatius (Plate III). A third, representing Saint Francis Borgia, has disappeared. These august figures, serene of

Saint Francis Xavier

countenance, their weighty habits shrouding
their forms, are typical of Fernández.
Even the affected grace of the hands is
present. A portion of Saint Francis
Xavier's ample cape sweeps across his
form. With a martial stride such as may
have carried him through the perils of
India he seems to advance, his eyes fixed
on the cross attached to the staff in his
right hand. His firm, strong features are
eloquent of the pioneer's force and the
zealot's fire.

*Saint
Ignatius of
Loyola*

The statue of Saint Ignatius on the
altar at the epistle side is a fitting companion to *Saint Francis Xavier*. The edges
of his cape, their lines broken by his
slightly outstretched hands, fall sharply
inward in the manner typical of this
sculptor, revealing the clumsy arrangement
of his habit. His right hand holds the
symbol of his order, the monogram IHS
surmounted by a cross and encircled by
rays, and the other a model of a church.
His face, gazing at the symbol, follows the
characteristics made familiar by portraits

PLATE XII

Photograph Hauser y Menet

DETAIL OF THE CRISTO DEL PARDO
Madrid. Convent of Capuchinos del Pardo

of the subject, — a face whose asceticism
is emphasized by the high, bald forehead
and furrowed cheeks. The attitude suggests rather the meditative recluse than
the leader of the church militant, but
there is evidence in the intensity of
his expression of that single-minded
ardour which shaped the great Jesuit
organization.

No documentary evidence is available
with regard to the sculptural part of the
retablo of the Monastery of *las Huelgas*,
Valladolid, attributed to Fernández, but
it is closely related in style to that of
the Church of *San Miguel*. The polychromy and painting, by a contract dated
May 9th, 1614, were assigned to Tomás de
Prado, the specifications stating that the
sculpture was then ready for the finishing
process. The images were to be gilded
and *estofado* (28). There are only minor
differences in structure between this and
the one in the Church of *San Miguel*.
Both are of two stories and an attic,
separated by unbroken entablatures, the

*Retablo
of the
Monastery
of las
Huelgas,
Valladolid*

main stories containing six columns each. The columns of the *retablo* of *las Huelgas*, instead of varying in the different stories, are all fluted Corinthian in style. The attic likewise consists of two central columns enclosing the Crucifixion, Virgin, and Saint John, flanked by coats of arms. This section is completed, instead of by figures of the evangelists, by Saint Michael and the Guardian Angel. In the central panel of the first story, replacing the tabernacle, is a relief, the figures almost in the round, representing Christ bending from the cross to embrace Saint Bernard. A canopy with a looped curtain frames the scene. The legend illustrated is mentioned in Rivadeneira (29), who says:

"And thus he [Saint Bernard] not only attained a very perfect habit of prayer and meditation, but also a very high degree of passive contemplation . . . And the Lord rewarded him to such a degree that one time when he was weeping before a crucifix, the Crucified One Himself stretched out His arm and laid it upon him,

PLATE XIII

CRISTO YACENTE
Madrid.   Church of San Plácido

embracing and caressing him with singular
favour."

Above this panel is the Assumption,
which shows the Virgin, enveloped in con-
fused draperies, surrounded by a mandorla
of jubilant cherubs. The outer niches contain statues of Saint John the Baptist,
Saint Joseph, and two other saints. Half-
figures in relief, perhaps fathers of the
church, take the place of paintings in the
square spaces above them. The other large
panels are occupied by paintings. On the
base, oblong reliefs representing the four
evangelists replace the Virtues of the *San
Miguel retablo*.

Not only is the frame similar to that of
the *retablo* of *San Miguel*, but the sculpture is very like that of the four saints in
the niches of the latter. The reliefs of
the four evangelists on the base are also
related in style to those of the four Virtues. This second *retablo* bears more evident marks of Fernández's handiwork. The
statues of saints with the folds of cloth
falling over the shoulder and with sudden

slanting folds at the bottom as if a gust of wind had caught them are comparable to those of the Eibar *retablo,* while the Crucifixion group of the attic is identical with those of the *retablos* of *San Miguel,* Vitoria, and Plasencia Cathedral. The angels also bear a certain kinship with the ones in these two *retablos.* What conclusions can one draw from this comparison? The sculpture of the *retablo* of *las Huelgas* may be accepted as Fernández's work with the possible collaboration of assistants. The *Saint Michael,* the statues in the side niches, and the reliefs of the base of the *retablo* of *San Miguel* may possibly be his. The frames of both *retablos,* undoubtedly conceived by the same mind, may be his, the differences between these and later ones indicating an early stage of development, or they may be the work of an *ensamblador* who himself designed them. There are in Medina del Campo two *retablos,* one of which (that of the Church of *Santiago*) is identical in structure with that of the Church of *San Miguel* and bears sculpture similar to the reliefs, the other (that of the Church of *San Facundo y San Primitivo*) akin to the one in the Monastery of *las Huelgas*. This similarity lends weight to the supposition that an *ensamblador* or group of *ensambladores* other than Fernández was responsible for all. Agapito y Revilla (30) states that Francisco Velázquez was the architect of the *retablo* of *las Huelgas*, basing his opinion on its similarity to that of the Convent of *Santa Isabel* constructed by this *ensamblador* in 1613, but since he gives no other authority for his statement, it cannot be accepted unreservedly. The date 1616 inscribed on the *retablo* of the Monastery of *las Huelgas* denotes its final completion.

Twelve years elapsed between the contract for the *retablo* of *San Miguel* and the next extant one, that for a Franciscan monastery in Vitoria. It was ordered by Mariana Vélez Ladrón de Guevara, countess of Triviana, the widow of Carlos de Alava, a member of the family who appear as his most important patrons. The Mon-

Retablo of the Franciscan monastery, Vitoria

Retablo
of the
Church of
San Miguel,
Vitoria

astery of *Nuestra Señora de la Concep-ción,* founded by the Countess in fulfillment of her husband's bequest, had just been completed, and on November 13th, 1618, Fernández was engaged for the sculpture of the *retablo* of the main altar and collaterals. In 1621 he received a total of 16,649 *reales* in payment. The altarpiece was of two stories, with the Immaculate Conception as the main theme.

That this work was successful seems proved by his engagement, three years later (1624), for the *retablo* of the Church of *San Miguel* in the same city (Plate IV). This *retablo* is an exemplar of the general type. It is of two stories and an attic, with the usual six fluted Corinthian columns in the main stories. Peculiarities of this *retablo* are the cartouches supported by cherubs which fill the spaces between the capitals of the columns enclosing the outer panels. The central figure of the first story, above the tabernacle, is the Immaculate Conception, with Saint Peter and Saint Paul on either side. Saint

PLATE XIV

Photograph Moreno

SAINT MONICA
Madrid. Convent of la Encarnación

Michael dominates the second story. A youthful warrior whose wings and fluttering draperies denote his kinship with the angels, he tramples underfoot a very small dragon. His amused smile bears witness to the ease of the conquest. At his left and right are Saint Sebastian and Saint Philip. Four large panels in the outer spaces depict the following scenes: on the lower story, the Nativity and the Circumcision; above these, two scenes from the miracle of Saint Michael on the Monte Gargano, one showing the arrow aimed at the bull returning to pierce the sender, and the other, Saint Michael appearing to the bishop and villagers to apprise them of the sanctity of the spot and his desire for a church there. The central panel of the attic contains the Crucifix accompanied by the Virgin and Saint John, with God the Father appearing above. The Virgin and Saint John are very closely related to their counterparts in the *retablos* of Plasencia Cathedral and the Monastery of *las Huelgas,* Valladolid. At

the left of the Crucifixion is Saint John
the Baptist, and at the right a saint who
is probably James the Great. Figures of
angels surmount the end columns of the
retablo. Narrow panels bearing reliefs
serve as bases for each story. Those at
the bottom represent the Annunciation,
the Adoration of the Magi, the Presenta-
tion in the Temple, and the Visitation. Between the first and second stories
are reliefs of the Latin fathers and the
evangelists, while below the attic appear
personifications of the cardinal virtues.
The pictorial quality of the reliefs, with
their massed figures and scenic accesso-
ries, is apparent. The Virtues of the attic
fill their stations with appropriate grace.
In the single statues there is a tendency
to an over-elaboration of folds to which
the sculptor's angular manner did not
readily lend itself. The carpentry was by
an *ensamblador* with the surname of Velázquez, variously cited with the forenames
of Juan, Diego, and Cristóbal. It could
not be the same man who made the frame

PLATE XV

Photograph Moreno

SAINT AUGUSTINE
Madrid. Convent of la Encarnación

of the *retablo* for the church of the same name in Valladolid, since he died in 1616. Agapito y Revilla (31) says that Juan Velázquez was the son of Cristóbal and cites him as *ensamblador* of this *retablo*, and, with his brother Francisco, of that of Plasencia Cathedral.

Ponz (32) states that Diego Valentín Díaz, who so often officiated as painter for Fernández's sculpture, performed that service here, in conjunction with Diego de la Peña. The division of the total cost of this work shows the comparative importance of the polychromy. For the sculpture and architecture there were expended 49,309 *reales* and 17 *maravedís*; for the gilding and painting, 29,988 *reales* and 5 *maravedís*; for the pedestal of black marble and white stone, 2,893 *reales*. The work was completed in 1632.

One of the principal subjects of this *retablo*, the Immaculate Conception, was a favourite theme in Spanish art at this period. Fernández seems to have originated this one type and to have repeated it

The Immaculate Conception

throughout his work. The original model
would seem to be the one made for the
Convent of *San Francisco,* Valladolid, in
1617, which was first placed in the Chapel
of the Count of Cabra, and then on the
retablo of the main altar. Bosarte's description (33) indicates that it was similar
to later examples. Of the one which figured in the *retablo* of the Franciscans at
Vitoria no description is available, but in
those of the *retablos* of *San Miguel,* Vitoria, and the Franciscan convent at
Eibar, the same type is apparent. Some
measure of that chivalric love which the
Middle Ages had squandered on fair ladies
seems to have been converted into devo-
tion for the Virgin as the perfect embodi-
ment of feminine grace, beauty, and virtue. The most intense expression of this
romantic ardour was concentrated in the
cult of Our Lady of the Immaculate Conception — a being of transcendent beauty
removed from all taint of earthly sin. Fernández interpreted this feeling in his version of the mystery. Her head is bent very

PLATE XVI

SAINT DOMINIC
Valladolid. Convent of San Pablo

slightly, her hair flowing smoothly over her shoulders, and her hands joined in the attitude of prayer. Her cloak falls in straight lines on both sides, its long folds interrupted only by small indentations towards the bottom. There is in this carefully balanced, static figure some sense of the mystical character of the subject. She is wrapt in a brooding calm, humble wonder at her own lofty station. No hieratic majesty obscures her tenderness, which a gentle dignity saves from too great sweetness.

As late as the eighteenth century copies were made of this type. Two in Valencia, that in the Chapel of *la Purísima Concepción* in the Cathedral by José Esteve y Bonet, and that in the *Colegio del Corpus Christi* attributed to Alonso Cano, repeat almost exactly Fernández's conception.

IV

In the large *retablos* containing an abundance of statues and reliefs, the individual pieces of sculpture must be subordinated to the general scheme, and the assistance of other sculptors must be sought. It is in the *retablos* for small altars, therefore, where the work is near at hand and entirely the master's own, that one must look for some of his most important work. It was in these that Fernández, following Juní's example, developed sculpture in the round. Since it was placed against the wall and was not intended to be viewed from all sides, it had still to be considered in relation to its background. These single representations, or a central group with perhaps two figures in side niches, gradually took the place, even on high altars, of the larger *retablos*.

One such in a chapel of the Church of *The Holy Family*
San Lorenzo at Valladolid, sculptured in
1621, represents the Holy Family. Saint
Joseph stands at the right, the Virgin at
the left, and the Christ Child between them.
Saint Joseph leans upon a staff held in his
left hand. The Virgin's right hand is
raised. Both gaze down at the Child
Jesus, who reaches up to take their hands.
The Virgin's mantle is caught at her right
shoulder, making long slanting folds, while
one end of Saint Joseph's cloak falls over
his left shoulder. The attitude which
Fernández affected, comparable to the
swing of certain French Gothic Virgins, is
well illustrated in these two statues. The
Child's figure, with its bunchy draperies
about the hips and at the feet, is not
agreeable, nor has the group as a whole
any particular charm.

This treatment of the Holy Family is unusual, since, although Saint Joseph is often
represented standing with the Child by his
side, he is seldom given equal prominence
with the Virgin in a group where she ap-

pears. The arrangement has a close parallel in a group of the Virgin and her parents
in the Valladolid Museum attributed to
Francisco del Rincón. The attribution is
too vague to warrant that conclusions be
drawn from it, but it may be another hint
of the artistic relationship between the
two sculptors, albeit no kinship in the
matter of technique is apparent.

The detailed instructions for the polychromy of *The Holy Family* are of value.
They follow:

" 'Conditions which must be observed
in painting the flesh tones and painting the
figures of Our Lady, the Child Jesus, and
Saint Joseph.

" 'In the first place the flesh tones of
all three figures must be mat, giving to
each one the flesh colour which is fitting
with regard to the subject, the Child like
a child and the Virgin similarly, imitating
in the flesh tones of Saint Joseph those of
a man, differentiating them as is most
suitable; painting the eyes on crystal and
touching up the hair of the image of the

PLATE XVII

SAINT IGNATIUS OF LOYOLA
Attributed to Fernández
Vergara. Seminary

Child with prepared gold (*oro molido*) and those of the saint with colour so that they resemble hair; the colours of the hair very pleasing and with all propriety throughout as befits the ages or carrying out the orders which Gregorio Fernandez may give and to the taste of the officials of this holy brotherhood. As to the garments it is stipulated that they are to be coloured in oil with the best colours which are to be found in Sebilla. The mantle of the image [of the Virgin] is to be blue, giving it at the edge some points of gold and a border of painting imitating embroidery touched up with prepared gold of the width and disposition which the aforesaid Gregorio Fernandez may direct on condition that it remain narrow in order to represent a light mantle. The robe is to be carmine which imitates a very fine purple and it too is to have its border, the richest and prettiest possible and touched up with prepared gold, and if it should seem advisable to G.° Fernandez and the officials of the aforesaid brotherhood to put on the mantle and robe some patterns in gold they shall be put on either at the edge or shall be those which form the border. The headdress of the image is to bear at the edge gold lacework and for a border is to imitate something like a chain stitch, or the whole thing reproducing a fabric which resembles gauze. On the girdle of the image shall be placed also gold lacework, the ends with their fringe, giving the girdle the prettiest colour possible and one which contrasts with the purple colour of the robe. As to the garment of the Child it is stipulated that it must be violet, the brightest and prettiest colour possible made from the aforesaid colours found in Sibilla, and likewise it is to have a border in the same form and manner although of different workmanship from that of His Mother, and the girdle of the Child shall have its gold lacework and fringe, and on the little sandals false pearls or something resembling embroidery. As to the garment of Saint Joseph the tunic shall be the brightest possible green made with great care using throughout the best and most fitting oils in order that the colours may not fade. The saint's mantle shall be yellow or if it should seem better from now until the time it is made, another colour. It and the tunic shall have their borders imitating embroidery and the whole touched up with prepared gold, and if to make the embroidery stand out it should seem advisable that the space occupied by the width of the border should be made of another colour, it shall be the most fitting, and the aforesaid Gregorio Fernandez shall decide as a person who wishes his figures to look well and to appear like works of his hands, and if all this should not be done to his taste and satisfaction he who undertook it shall neither be considered to have fulfilled his contract nor shall he be paid. All the aforementioned must be done by the day of Saint Joseph of this year 1621 provided that the sculpture is finished a month before the celebration. . . The

crystal eyes, gold edgings and trimmings
if they should be used, the aforesaid
brotherhood must provide and must bring
the colours from Sivilla, paying whoever
may be given this commission what they
cost in Sivilla . . .'" (34).
Signed by Diego Balentin Diaz [sic] and
Gregorio Fernandez [sic]. The figures
have since been repainted.

In this scheme of polychromy the turn
toward simplicity is apparent. The use of
gold in the imitation of rich brocades had
reached its apogee and had become a mere
convention. Juní had used less gold but
had combined his colours in riotous profusion. Fernández sobered all this, having garments painted in solid colours re-
lieved only by borders patterned in gold,
perhaps with another colour as a background for the gold. Some use of garments
estofado still persisted, but in a small proportion. Although he did not polychrome
his own works, the deference to his opinions
shown in this contract proves that the
painting and gilding must have been done

PLATE XVIII

THE REPENTANT MAGDALENE
Valladolid. Church of San Miguel

under his supervision and in pursuance of
his ideas.

Among the subjects to which Spanish *Mater*
artists were especially attracted, because *Dolorosa*
of the depth of emotion involved, was the *(Valladolid.*
Mater Dolorosa. The most important of *La Cruz)*
these by Fernández is that in the Church
of *la Cruz,* Valladolid (Plate V). The
Virgin is seated on a rock, both arms out-
spread, her face upturned, a posture repeated in the *Pietà* of the Church of *San
Martín,* Valladolid. Although this statue
may be adequate for devotional needs, it
hardly merits M. Dieulafoy's opinion that
it is " The masterpiece of Gregorio Hernandez, perhaps even the masterpiece of
polychrome statuary, if one limits oneself
to the schools of the north . . ." (35).
The outstretched arms, rigid in their bulky
sleeves, give no semblance of life or movement. The upper part of the figure seems
to have no connection with the lower. The
face alone redeems the image. A type
which Fernández used again and again, it
is one of great regularity and dignity.

It is rather oblong than oval, the cheeks
slightly hollowed. The eyes are set far
apart beneath a broad forehead. The
nose is straight, and the lips are finely
chiseled. It recalls strongly, although refined by centuries of civilization, that
Greco-Phœnician ideal immortalized in the
Lady of Elche. It is difficult to judge
what the original polychromy may have
been since Bosarte (36), Sangrador Vitores (37), and others state that the figure
has been repainted by an unskillful hand
and the glass tears added. Dieulafoy (38)
describes the present colouring as follows:

"The deep eyes outlined by dark circles
form two tragic spots in the pale face
with its bloodless lips. A gray cape with
a simple white fillet at the edge, and below the cape a veil of cream-coloured
muslin edged with a very fine black line
surround the face, and, by a contrast of
very light tints which envelop it, it thus
takes on an airy, celestial aspect, while
the brown robe with blood-red reflections
and the note of yellow ochre in the revers

of the sleeves bring the thought back to earth. A blue-black drapery whose gloom is in accord with the grief of the Virgin falls in ample folds to the ground like a mourning cloak."

This statue inevitably invites comparison with the similar one by Juní in the Church of *las Angustias*. The latter is even more dramatic, the right hand clutched to the breast, the draperies swirling like the eddies of a swift current. The face Fernández might easily have derived from his predecessor, but he has purified the outlines and refined the expression. The arrangement of the lower part of the draperies, irregular and twisted, has a strong suggestion of Juní.

In the *Museo Provincial* there is another figure, apparently a Mater Dolorosa (Plate VI), which may once have formed part of a Crucifixion group. Serrano Fatigati (39) rejects its authenticity for what seem insufficient reasons, although it is somewhat heavily proportioned. The Virgin stands with her hands clasped at her breast and

Mater Dolorosa (Valladolid. Museo Provincial)

her face turned upward. A corner of her mantle is draped over her left arm, a familiar expedient with Fernández, and her robe is confined by a girdle tied in a looped knot similar to those visible in mortuary statues of the sixteenth century. The face is the same type which appears in the *Pietà* of the *Museo Provincial* and in the *Mater Dolorosa* of the Church of *la Cruz.*

Saint Mary Magdalene, supposedly a companion to the preceding statue, seems more akin to the processional figures than to Fernández's other work. The arrangement of the hair, rolled back from the forehead on each side, repeats that of the Magdalene in the *paso* of *The Descent from the Cross,* while the cloak wound about the form resembles those of the *Saint Veronica* of the *paso* of *Christ Bearing the Cross* and of another Magdalene in the Church of *las Angustias.* The inferiority of this image relegates it to the rank of a school work.

The Pietà may be considered as an

Saint Mary Magdalene

PLATE XIX

RETABLO MAYOR
Eibar. Convent of Franciscas

elaboration of the theme of the Mater Dolorosa. This scene, together with the others representing the Passion of Christ, was peculiarly appropriate to Spanish art since it dwelt on the human, tangible theme of suffering and death. Indeed, the first step which Saint Theresa recommended for the perfection of prayer was an imaginative re-creation of the Passion. Fernández produced two versions of the Pietà — one in the *Museo Provincial* and one in the Church of *San Martín* at Valladolid. The one in the *Museo Provincial* (Plate VII), originally in the Church of *las Angustias,* is justly the most celebrated of Fernández's works. Only the shoulders of Christ are supported in the Virgin's embrace; the rest of his body, protected by a sheet, reclines upon a rocky slope. The upward trend of the broad folds over the Virgin's knee and of the Saviour's arm flung across it, interrupted for a moment by the despairing grip of her hand on His arm, are brought to a climax in her uplifted face. Her right

Pietà (Valladolid. Museo Provincial)

hand breaks the flowing lines of the figures
and draperies in a sudden, arresting gesture of appeal. Her face is not strident
in its grief, but is an expression of sheer
human anguish and despair, the brow contracted in pain, the eyes swollen with weeping, the lips gasping for breath. In spite
of the realism of these details, the head
is an ideal conception of a woman, mature,
but not old, her face unmarred either
by age or suffering. Her countenance is
framed by a white wimple, while the blue
mantle above casts a tragic shadow.

All the bitterness of death is concentrated in the Mother's sorrow. No trace of
horror or suffering lingers about the
Saviour's form. His body seems relaxed
not so much in death as in complete and
grateful repose. The head alone lacks the
absolute inertia which would make it accord with the rest of the figure. Far
removed as this sculptor is from the spirit
of the Italian Renaissance, its example and
influence seem not to have been entirely
lost, for in this representation of Christ,

slim and elegant, the limbs composed with
calm grace, there is nothing of the racked
emaciation of the work of the Gothic
masters nor yet of the violent naturalism
of those who were to follow. The face,
long and narrow, with high cheek-bones,
straight nose, and pointed chin, seems
based somewhat on traditional representations and somewhat on actual types. The
hair displays Fernández's usual treatment,
thick strands quite separate from each
other. The regular undulations and careful
arrangement are often, as in this instance,
a detriment. Hollow cheeks and weary
lids over sunken eyes tell of pain, now
ended.

The second *Pietà* in Valladolid (Plate
VIII) was made for the Convent of *San
Francisco*. It was in a chapel under the
patronage of private persons, and at the
dispersion of that congregation was transferred to a chapel owned by the same
families, the Salcedos and Rivas, in the
Church of *San Martín*. That this is an
authentic work by Fernández is attested

Pietà
(Valladolid.
San Martín)

by the monk Matías de Sobremonte (40)
in his contemporary history of the Convent of *San Francisco*. The grouping may
be referred to the *Pietà* which forms part
of the *retablo* of the Church of *las Angustias,* Valladolid, executed in 1600 by
Cristóbal Velázquez, although the latter
is Italian in technique. In view of the
intimate relations which existed between
the two men, it is legitimate to suppose
that Fernández took his idea from the
work of the man who often acted as his
ensamblador. The Virgin, at the foot of
the Cross, rests upon one knee, both arms
outstretched, and her head turned towards
the left. The form of Christ, seated on
the ground at her knee, is propped
against her. His right arm is flung over
her knee; the other lies at His side. His
head has sunk forward. The background
is a painted landscape with a stream,
buildings, and trees. This group is ugly
with the ugliness of suffering itself. No
sense of the deeper significance of the
scene palliates its grim reality. It is a

PLATE XX

MATER DOLOROSA
Attributed to Fernández
Vitoria. Church of San Pedro

crushed, pathetic figure, crumpled on the ground; the agonized face lifted above it, that of a distracted mother.

An example in the *Carmen Descalzo* at Burgos (Plate IX) is attributed to him without question by the Count de la Viñaza (41) and Bosarte (42) and is said by Tormo (43) to be at least of his school, but the attribution is ill-considered. The composition is very like that of the one in the Church of *San Martín,* but this is a work of much greater appeal. There are the same attitudes, — the Virgin's eyes and her outstretched arms turned towards heaven, the body of Christ resting against His Mother's knee, — but the repetition is not exact. The head of the Virgin is turned to the right, the body of Christ raised to a less cramped position, more gracefully arranged. His figure is more robust than is typical of Fernández, and although the Virgin's face is of a baf-flingly similar type, the more delicate out-lines of the features serve to distinguish it. There is more animation and variety

Pietà (Burgos. Carmen Descalzo)

in the gesture of her hands than Fernández managed to convey either in the *Pietà* of the Church of *San Martín* or in the *Mater Dolorosa* of the Church of *la Cruz*. The draperies have none of the sharp angles and sudden breaks used by Fernández. From it breathes a gentler spirit than the stark tragedy which Fernández conjured up.

Christ at the Column (Valladolid. La Cruz)

The representations of Christ form a long and imposing array composed chiefly of events of the Passion. A *Christ at the Column* in the Church of *la Cruz*, Valladolid (Plate X), is probably the original model from which many variants were made. The left foot is slightly advanced. The head is somewhat bowed, but the eyes are directed at the persecutors. The left hand rests on the column with the right tied to it at the wrist, the hand uplifted, and the fingers spread in a gesture of affected grace. The delicate contours of the limbs, the shrinking shoulders, the slender fingers, verge on effeminacy. The loin cloth projects from the body with unnatural stiffness. Distress is expressed by the exaggerated upturning of the eyes, showing the white below the pupils. The hair is arranged in the same neat fashion as that of the Christ in the *Pietà* of the *Museo Provincial*. This conception seems to have gained popular approbation, judging from the legend which is associated with it. For it is related that when Fernández was looking upon the completed figure, his mind stirred by a deep exaltation, it opened its lips and spoke, saying, "Where didst thou behold me that hast portrayed me so well?" To this the sculptor replied, "Lord, in my heart" (44).

The most interesting variant is in the Convent of *Santa Teresa,* Avila. Although the posture is the same, the loin cloth is arranged with greater symmetry. The face arouses doubt as to Fernández's authorship because it is less elongated, the chin round instead of pointed, and the features softer. The hair falls in a mass on one shoulder like that of the Christ in the *Pietà* of the Church of *San Martín*.

Christ at the Column (Avila. Santa Teresa)

Cristo de la
Luz

Of crucifixes, aside from those forming parts of *retablos,* the number is surprisingly small. The one which has acquired greatest fame is the *Cristo de la Luz* in the *Museo Provincial* at Valladolid (Plate XI), formerly in the Monastery of *San Benito el Real.* It is not less stirring because of its quietude. The form which hangs on the cross seems lost in its own woe. There is no distortion, no violence in the attitude. The face alone, by its very vividness, expresses the full horror of the deed. There is grim reality in the sagging head with its sunken cheeks and closed eyes. A fold of the twisted loin cloth stands out sharply from the body, a peculiarity often repeated by Fernández.

Cristo del
Conjo

Another crucifix attributed to him adorns the parish church of Conjo, near Santiago de Compostela, having been taken from the Convent of *Mercenarios Calzados* of that city. It is similar to the *Cristo de la Luz* but has been defaced by the addition of false hair and beard and the replacing of the carved draperies by some of actual

PLATE XXI

SAINT THERESA
Valladolid. Museo Provincial de Bellas Artes

cloth. Still another example attributed to *Cristo de los Trabajos*
him, known as the *Cristo de los Trabajos*,
reverenced in the parish church of Laguna
de Duero, according to the parish records,
was brought from Valladolid in 1813 because it was in a place where it suffered
from neglect and improper treatment.
Martí (45) states that it resembles the
Cristo de la Luz, although the forms are
fuller.

An aspect of the Saviour which gave rise *Cristos Yacentes*
to many repetitions was that of the Christ
lying on the tomb, the *Cristo Yacente.*
Abhorrent as these sanguinary sculptures
are to many minds, their creation is rooted
in the feeling expressed in the famous
sonnet:

" I am not moved to love Thee, O my
    Lord,
  By any longing for Thy Promised
    Land;
  Nor by the fear of Hell am I un-
    manned
  To cease from my transgressing deed
    or word.

'Tis Thou Thyself dost move me, —
   Thy blood poured
Upon the cross from nailèd foot and
   hand;
And all the wounds that did Thy body
   brand;
And all Thy shame and bitter death's
   award " (46).

These recumbent figures are all, to a large extent, repetitions of the same model with slight variations, the treatment of the head showing the greatest divergence. Five attributed to Fernández are in Madrid, while various copies are scattered through the churches, convents, and monasteries of Valladolid.

Cristo del Pardo

Of them all the *Cristo del Pardo* (Plate XII), in the Capuchin Convent of the Pardo, is probably the precursor. It was ordered by Philip the Third on April 8th, 1605, being thus contemporaneous with the decorative statues which are Fernández's first recorded work. A comparison with Juní's figure of Christ in *The Entombment*

PLATE XXII

SAINT THERESA
Avila. Convent of Santa Teresa

of Segovia Cathedral reveals striking
similarities, — and just as striking differences. For although the left knee is
slightly lifted, resting against the right, in
the same fashion in both, although a
similar fold of the drapery falls across the
loins, although the shoulders are raised
and the head turned towards the front,
the arms lying limply at the sides; in
Juní's work each one of these details, by
a slight exaggeration, tends towards a dramatic feeling of sudden relaxation, of a
limp body abruptly flung down; in Fernández's depiction all is measured repose,
the hair spread carefully on the pillow,
the right arm lying smoothly at the side,
the left falling naturally upon the drapery.
The head, with half-closed, sunken eyes,
the brow still slightly contracted, the
cheeks drawn, and the lips parted, is an
epitome of suffering.

The *Cristo Yacente* in the Church of
San Plácido (Plate XIII), although reputed by Mesonero Romanos (47) a
repetition by Pereira of the *Cristo del*

*Cristo
Yacente
(Madrid.
San Plácido)*

Pardo, bears evident marks of Fernández's handiwork. The elegant composure of the limbs, the narrow face and delicate features, all bespeak his authorship. One notices in Fernández's modeling of Christ's face the high bridge of the nose, the straight brows, the symmetrical depression about the eyeballs, the prominent cheekbones, and the easy merging of the full lips into the planes of the cheeks. All these details are present here. The one in the Prado (formerly in the Churches of *San Felipe Neri* and the *Buen Suceso*), although somewhat more robust, exhibits similar characteristics.

Saint Monica and Saint Augustine

A noble company of saints was that which Fernández marshaled in his procession. A host of them preside over every *retablo* which he composed and also adorn individual altars. Among the latter there are in the Convent of *la Encarnación,* Madrid, a *Saint Monica* (Plate XIV) and a *Saint Augustine* (Plate XV), at the right and left of the high altar. Saint Monica stands with her weight on her right foot.

She gazes at a crucifix held in her right hand, while her left holds a heavy book under which the cape of her Augustinian habit is caught. Her girdle is fastened by a buckle. Her face is very like the *Mater Dolorosa* of the Church of *la Cruz,* Valladolid, as are also the deep folds of her cape, somewhat softer than usual. Saint Augustine carries a church placed on a book in his left hand, and in his right, a crozier. The patriarchal aspect of this saint with the long beard and piercing eyes is increased by his towering mitre and the long lines of his cope, swinging inward at the bottom. Both these figures have been repainted.

It was to another Madrid convent, that *Saint Anne* of the Carmelites, that there was taken an image of Saint Anne, carried on men's shoulders all the way from Valladolid. This must have been an early production, since it was ordered by the sovereigns for the *Congregación de Correos* during their stay in Valladolid, and was transferred at the time of the removal of the Court.

These notices were derived from a Carmelite historian (48), but it is not known
whether the statue still exists.

Saint
Dominic

　　The Convent of *San Pablo,* in Valladolid,
contains in the Chapel of *Santo Domingo*
an altarpiece by Fernández (Plate XVI)
which was ordered, probably in 1626, by
Baltasar Navarrete, a noted theologian of
Valladolid, at one time prior of the convent. Saint Dominic, the only figure, half
kneels on a group of clouds. The crucifix
upraised in his left hand is the object of
his fervent adoration. His right hand holds
a lily.　The approach of the baroque
period is foreshadowed in the cluttered
folds of the habit about his feet.　The
cape thrown back by his uplifted arms
masses bulkily about his shoulders, while
small transverse indentations towards the
lower edge add to the chaos below. The
powerful face, the brow slightly contracted
by concentration, seems to be gathering
inspiration for a burst of eloquent preach-
ing. It has the full, firm outlines dear to
Fernández. The base bears a typical orna-

PLATE XXIII

SAINT MARY MAGDALENE OF PAZZI
Valladolid. Museo Provincial de Bellas Artes

mentation of bars, rectangles, and lozenges in relief.

A striking parallel to the figures on the side altars of the Church of *San Miguel*, Valladolid, exists in a statue of Saint Ignatius in the chapel of the seminary at Vergara (Plate XVII). The attitude is like that of the *Saint Francis Xavier*. The saint has stopped to fix his attention on the symbol of his order held in his right hand. A corner of his cape is brought across his form and caught under the heavy book held in his left hand. The garments are more billowing, flow with smoother continuity, with less sharply broken folds and fewer broad planes, although they are not far removed in character from those of the *Saint Monica*. But in the face, when compared with that of the *Saint Ignatius* of the Church of *San Miguel*, one perceives a degree of characterization which gives the latter the appearance of a lay figure. The shape of the head, the modeling of the features are entirely different and can by no means be ascribed to Fernández.

Saint Ignatius of Loyola (Vergara. Seminary)

Saint
Sebastian

A *Saint Sebastian* in the *Museo Provin-cial*, Valladolid, sometimes attributed to Fernández, is probably only a school work. A comparison with the one forming part of the *retablo* of *San Miguel*, Vitoria, shows the differences in treatment. The one in the museum is a heavier figure, the face older and more distorted. The fingers are arched in an unnatural manner. The gnarled limbs of the tree behind him form a grotesque silhouette.

The
Repentant
Magdalene

One of the works upon which rests the fame of Pedro de Mena y Medrano, Malagan sculptor of the late seventeenth century, is a figure of the Magdalene contemplating a crucifix. She is clad only in a strip of matting held by a rope at the waist, and her hair is loose upon her shoulders. The prototype of this statue is to be found in one by Gregorio Fernández in the Church of *San Miguel* at Valladolid (Plate XVIII). This saint of Fernández's is of a less monumental type than his Virgins, although she is still considerably less wasted by abnegation than the examples which were to follow. Loving care has been expended in modeling the slightly knit brows, the downcast eyes, and sensitive mouth. Although there is not yet the exalted fervour of repentance which is reached in Mena's masterpiece, no less effective is the tenderness, the quiet sadness of the saint.

V

With all this host of isolated statues Fernández did not cease carving large *retablos* but rather produced them with increasing frequency. A large number of commissions were assigned to him by or through the influence of Juan de Orbea, a monk in the Convent of the *Carmen Calzado* at Valladolid and a nephew of that Countess of Triviana who had ordered, in 1618, the *retablo* for the Franciscan monastery at Vitoria. This family seem to have been the sculptor's only patrons from among the nobility, if the fleeting notice of the royal family be excepted. In 1624, two years before Fernández carved the *retablo* of *Santo Domingo,* a long correspondence passed between Juan de Orbea and Juan López de Issasi, son of the founders of the Convent of Franciscan Nuns at Eibar, whose family are described

in a document quoted in Martí (49) as
" ' close relatives of . . . Juan de Orbea.' "
The topic of this series of letters was the
retablo for the convent, for which Issasi
was then treating with a sculptor of that
vicinity, Pedro de Ayala by name. Juan
de Orbea, doubtful of the abilities of the
Guipuzcoan artisan, at first urged that at
least the gilding and polychromy be done
by men from Valladolid and suggested
that " ' The image of the Conception
Gregorio Hernandez would make very ad-
mirably because he is so much my friend
that he will put all his ability to it ' " (50).
López de Issasi, in reply, assented to his
friend's request that Fernández make the
figure of the Conception but did not wish
to give him the contract for the whole
retablo, offering as excuse the fact that
Fernández was so much sought after and
would probably want a higher price than
he wished to pay. He had already selected
one design of Pedro de Ayala's, " ' . . .
because in addition to the principal feasts
of *Our Lady* there appear in the *retablo*

Saint Joseph and the *Golden Gate of Saint Joachim and Saint Anne'* " (51). This plan he seems to have sent to Fray Juan, for in the latter's next letter he speaks in scornful terms of Ayala's design and urges with renewed vigour the engagement of Fernández for the whole work, giving assurance that the sculptor would do it conscientiously and would go himself to see that it was properly installed. The urgent advocacy of the Valladolid friar seems to have accomplished its purpose, since a letter from him written in 1629 mentions that he has paid Fernández a portion of what is due him and that the sculptor is then engaged on the *retablos* for the side altars.

The framework of the *retablo* (Plate XIX) is of the usual type, although of three stories and an attic instead of two. The columns are fluted Corinthian. The first story has been modernized, but in the centre of the second, under a round arch, is placed the Immaculate Conception, the loveliest example of this subject which

PLATE XXIV

THE BAPTISM OF CHRIST

Valladolid. Museo Provincial de Bellas Artes

Fernández created. Saint Paul and Saint
Peter serve as the Virgin's bodyguards,
while in the wide outer spaces are reliefs
representing the Annunciation and the
Visitation. Above the Virgin is Saint
Francis, a rather heavy and uninspired
conception. On either side of him is another saint; one, with a king's robes and
crown, may be Saint Hermengild. The two
reliefs of this story depict the Marriage
of the Virgin and a scene in which an angel
appears to a dying person. The attic contains the Crucifixion with God the Father
appearing above it. Contrary to the usual
scheme, Saint John and the Virgin occupy
separate niches. The former, although
seated and facing in an opposite direction,
repeats the same turn of the head and
gesture of the arm which appear in the
statues of Saint John of the *retablos* of
Plasencia Cathedral, the Church of *San
Miguel*, Vitoria, and the Monastery of *las
Huelgas*, Valladolid. The end columns are
completed by pinnacles, and coats of arms
are placed above the panels. The bases

below the reliefs and the pedestals of the columns are without ornamentation, and the broken pediment above Saint Francis's niche is lacking. Garlands are swung between the columns above the niches, and the panels are framed by a moulding bearing a typical decoration of alternate lozenges and double bars. The brackets supporting the statues are similar to those in the *retablo* of the Church of *San Miguel,* Vitoria. This *retablo* is distinguished from others by the same artist through its simplicity of design. The panels are not crowded with figures in haphazard juxtaposition but are grouped in pleasing patterns. The simple architectural settings are a grateful relief from too elaborate landscapes. Saint Peter's mantle has the end thrown over the shoulder in the typical manner, but there is noticeable an unusual roundness in the folds, especially where they slant toward the hems of the robes. The scene of the Annunciation is almost a literal repetition of a version of the same episode which appears in the *retablo mayor* of the Church of *Santa María,* Tudela de Duero, while the reliefs of seated saints on the base of the latter are comparable to those in the *retablo* of *San Miguel,* Valladolid. The plan of the Tudela de Duero *retablo* corresponds closely to that used by Fernández, but its exact connection with his work cannot now be determined. In 1613 it was being painted by artists from Valladolid.

A counterpart of the Mater Dolorosa in the attic of the Eibar *retablo* is in the Church of *San Pedro,* Vitoria (Plate XX). Her garments are gathered closely about her, and her head is bowed on a portion of her cloak held in her left hand. The oval face is marked by an expression of patient and controlled grief. It is conceivable that Fernández might have created several versions of the Mater Dolorosa, although fertility of invention is not one of his distinguishing characteristics, were it not that the figure is so far removed in spirit from the rest of his work. There are also technical differences in spite

Mater Dolorosa (Vitoria. San Pedro)

of a certain feeling of similarity. The folds lie smoothly, accentuating the pathetic droop of the head, although they have the typical short, transverse breaks. The hands are softly modeled; they sink into the drapery instead of standing out distinct and clear. The face is quite narrow, and although the full lips and fleshiness of the eyelids recall Fernández, the soft round outlines of the cheek and chin deny his touch. A comparison with the *Saint Veronica* of the *paso* of *Christ Bearing the Cross* and *The Repentant Magdalene* of the Church of *San Miguel*, Valladolid, nearest to this in type of face, will show these differences. The documentation of the Eibar *retablo* is not entirely convincing, since it does not state clearly that Fernández was finally chosen for the whole work, nor who were his assistants. Pedro de Ayala, who was first consulted concerning its plan, was a native of Vitoria. The idea is suggested that he may have had a share in its final composition and may also be responsible for this figure.

This hypothesis would account for the peculiarities in style already noted.

The interest of the monk of the *Carmen Calzado* did not cease with the Eibar *retablo,* since several of the numerous works by Fernández in that monastery were directly ordered by him. In 1627, at his instance, the patronage of the Chapel of *Santa Teresa* was ceded to the Countess of Triviana, his aunt. This disposition was granted in view of the bounty which he had displayed toward the convent with money derived from the bequest of the Countess of Oñate, likewise his aunt. For the *retablo* of this chapel he ordered from Fernández the figure of the saint, now in the *Museo Provincial* (Plate XXI). She stands clad in the habit of the Carmelite order, her left foot slightly advanced. Her left hand should hold a book, her right hand a pen poised ready to write. She inclines her head to catch the intonations of the Divine Spirit. The garments are painted in solid colours, the cape with a wide border. It falls heavily

Saint Theresa (Valladolid. Museo Provincial)

from her shoulders, the right side turned inward by its own weight and the left with a transverse fold which must have been originally caught under the book. A replica in Alcalá de Henares shows the proper position. Double bars, rectangles, and lozenges in relief adorn the base.

Saint Theresa (Avila. Santa Teresa)

A kneeling statue of this saint in the Convent of *Santa Teresa* of Avila (Plate XXII), in the chapel erected on the site of the room where she was born, represents her in an attitude of rapt adoration. Her left hand is at her breast as if to quell the emotion within, while her right hand is slightly extended in wonder at the vision. Her habit clings to her right side, recalling the similar arrangement in the gown of the Virgin who bestows the scapulary on Saint Simon Stock. A cape of real cloth has been added. The face, as is fitting in dealing with a real person rather than an ideal conception, is more human than those of the Virgins created by Fernández. Indeed, the hollows of the cheeks, the fold of flesh under the chin are characteristic

PLATE XXV

RETABLO MAYOR
Attributed to Fernández
Cegama. Parroquia

of the face of a middle-aged woman, in which one can trace some slight resemblance to actual portraits of the saint. A comparison with the statue in the museum at Valladolid is not unfavourable to this example. The posture, although dramatic, has less of artificial grace and more of spontaneity, while the greater mobility of the face conveys some sense of the stir of inward emotion.

Nor was Fray Juan content in endowing his convent with this one figure. The chapter graciously conceded him (in 1627) the privilege of embellishing the Chapel of *Nuestra Señora del Carmen* with her image, the Child in her arms, which has now been transferred to a chapel in the province of Ciudad Real. This statue is signalized by Ceán Bermúdez (52) as " the best by the hand of this artist which is known." The frequent appearance of the subject testifies to the popularity of its prototype.

Whether or not this same friar was instrumental in procuring further commis-

Virgen del Carmen

Retablo
of the
Convent
of the
*Carmen
Calzado,*
Valladolid

sions for the sculptor, much more of
Fernández's work was done for this Convent of the *Carmen Calzado,* and it was
here that he had his family tomb. On the
main altar there was a *retablo* by him
described by Bosarte (53) as being of two
stories. The first, of four Corinthian
columns, contained in the central space a
relief of the Virgin giving the scapulary to
Saint Simon Stock (54), and in the side
niches Saint Cyril of Jerusalem and Saint
Cyril of Alexandria. The attic was occupied, as in so many instances, by the
Crucifix with the Virgin and Saint John.
The central relief, now preserved in the
Museo Provincial, consists of figures
almost in the round attached to a flat
background amid an unpleasant confusion
of suspended cherubs and attentive angels.
The lack of design of the composition as
a whole is compensated for in some measure by the charm of the individual figures.
The Virgin, from her seat among the
clouds in the upper right-hand corner,
bends with a gracious dignity towards her

PLATE XXVI

RETABLO MAYOR
Attributed to Fernández
Oñate. Church of las Isabelas

servitor below, who, in his turn, receives the gift with due humility. The Christ Child held on His Mother's knee is rather a winsome figure. Below Him is seated the infant Saint John. The two angels standing, one at the left and one at the right of Saint Simon, are stiff figures in tunics with ugly, bunchy folds. No less inferior are the three angel musicians ensconced on clouds in the upper left-hand corner, although the instruments they hold are like those on which the elders in the Porch of Glory at Santiago Cathedral accompany their chants in praise of their King. The stiffness of the garments is not accentuated in the figure of the Virgin although her cape folds inward at the bottom with that same impression of inflexibility. Here again, the inequality of the workmanship prompts the inference that the secondary details were the work of pupils.

One other figure by Fernández from this sanctuary, now in the *Museo Provincial*, remains to be mentioned. It is Saint

Saint Mary Magdalene of Pazzi

Mary Magdalene of Pazzi (Plate XXIII) kneeling in contemplation of a crucifix in her left hand. The heavy cape of the Carmelite habit falls over her arms. Her head, the face framed in a white wimple, is covered by a dark cloth; where the scapulary covers the breast a hollow framed by cherubs' heads has been made to form a reliquary. The garments are treated with great simplicity: broad surfaces and long, deep folds. Her features are of the noble type so frequently repeated. It is as if the artist had visualized the moment in her life when " . . . upon receiving the crucifix in her hands . . . she felt her soul united with Christ through love with such spiritual sweetness that she confessed that it was the greatest she had felt up to that time, and she felt Christ like a loadstone drawing her heart, so that she protested that she loved no other thing in life but Christ " (55).

The artist's health was already broken when he undertook the sculpture for the

retablo mayor of the Cathedral of Plasencia. A letter written from Valladolid,
March 25th, 1629, by the licentiate Juan
Cabeza Leal, representing the Cathedral
Chapter, reports his progress at that date.
At the instance of the Chapter the author
of the letter urged Fernández, who was
working on the base, to leave that and
complete first the main scene, that of the
Assumption, so that in the event of his
sudden death, the principal part, at least,
would be by the master's hand. The
letter is loud in praise of the artist and
censures the action of some of the canons
who, on their own responsibility, had written to the sculptor to chide him for his
delay. The *retablo* was finished during
his lifetime. It is more elaborate than is
usual, consisting of two main stories with
eight Corinthian columns each, and an attic
with four similar ones. The main composition occupies the central panel of the
second story and represents the Assumption in figures more than life-size. In the
corresponding space of the first story is

the tabernacle. In the centre of the attic
is the Crucifixion with the Virgin, Saint
John, and the Magdalene — her inclusion
an innovation — , the scene surmounted by
a relief of God the Father. Figures of angels and personifications of virtues complete
this story. The remaining four large panels
are occupied by paintings by Francisco
Rizi. The saints in their niches are ap-
propriately paired: two apostles, Saint
Peter and Saint Paul, stand guard over the
tabernacle, Saint Paul very like his counterpart in the *retablo* of *San Miguel,* Valladolid; beyond them, Saint John the
Baptist and Saint James the Great; beside
the Assumption of the Virgin, Saint
Joachim and Saint Anne, the latter,
although in a reversed position, showing
a close affinity to the Virgin of *The Holy
Family* in the Church of *San Lorenzo,*
Valladolid; in the outer spaces of this
story, Saints Fulgence and Florentina,
brother and sister, the latter patroness of
the diocese of Plasencia; in the attic,
Saint Theresa, a repetition of the figure in

PLATE XXVII

PASO OF THE FLAGELLATION

With figures by or attributed to Fernández.
Christ at the Column from the Church of *la Cruz*,
Valladolid; other figures from the *Museo Provincial
de Bellas Artes*

the Valladolid museum, and Saint Joseph,
to whom she was especially devoted. The
bases of the first story are decorated with
bas-reliefs of scenes from the Passion of
Christ, and those of the second with similar reliefs from the life of the Virgin.
The pedestals of the columns of both
stories bear reliefs of doctors of the
church, evangelists, and saints. The bases
and pedestals of the attic bear a painted
ornamentation. Garlands at the heads of
the niches and borders of alternating ovals
and lozenges around the panels are again
present. The desultory baroque tendencies
of Fernández's sculpture are well illustrated in the relief of the Assumption.
The figures are not confined within the
frame but overflow its borders. Above
the seething mass of apostles Our Lady,
angel-guided, "soars into realms of light".
Although she is related to the Virgins of
the Immaculate Conception, there is more
motion in the folds of her cape.

In contrast with the calm dignity of
the saints, the angels are full of motion.

Their garments are stirred by all the winds of their heavenly domain and swept against their limbs. Whether they appear in the round or in relief, Fernández always distinguishes his angels in this way. The skirts of such unpretentious beings as those in the scene of the bestowal of the scapulary on Saint Simon Stock are faintly ruffled as if still disturbed by their flight through space.

Benavides (56), *chantre* of Plasencia Cathedral, states that the *retablo* was ordered in 1624 and that the *ensambladores* were the brothers Juan and Cristóbal Velázquez of Valladolid. Since the latter died in 1616, the note cannot be accepted as trustworthy. Agapito y Revilla (57), while quoting the same date, gives the names of the architects as Francisco and Juan Velázquez, brothers. Here, again, one is troubled by lack of authority for the statement.

At this same period Fernández was carrying out another important commission, the *retablo* for the Sanctuary of

Nuestra Señora de Aránzazu, which was begun in 1627 and completed before his death. The officials of this convent, no less concerned for the state of the sculptor's health than were those of Plasencia, paid him five hundred *ducados* on account in February, 1635, in order that he might consider himself under still greater obligations to hasten the work. He had undertaken the sculpture of the *retablo* and the choir stalls without a definite statement of the price, it being stipulated that the value should be ascertained after the work was finished. In order that he might have money to carry it on, he was to receive on account a thousand *ducados* when he undertook the work and five hundred *ducados* every year after that. This annual stipend was duly paid for five years. In 1633, however, the *Guardián* was compelled by the trustees to stop work on the sanctuary until the twenty-three thousand, thirty-eight masses which the community owed had been celebrated. Therefore in 1635 the work was resumed. The *Guardián*

Retablo of the Sanctuary of Nuestra Señora de Aránzazu

went to Valladolid to ask Fernández to set a price on his work. This the latter was unwilling to do, wishing to have it evaluated for his greater profit, but finally stated that it was worth more than ten thousand *ducados*. The *Guardián* at length agreed to pay him within two years four thousand *ducados* in addition to the thirty-five hundred which he had already received. When Fernández decided that he was too busy to undertake the choir stalls, they were assigned (in 1630) to a sculptor of Cegama, Juan García de Verástegui, Fernández doing only the stall of the *Guardián* and the *tarjetas* of the upper range. All these works seem to have perished in a conflagration during the Carlist wars.

Retablos of the Benedictine monastery, Sahagún

At the time of his death Fernández was occupied with two *retablos* for the Benedictine monastery of Sahagún. The statue of Saint Benedict, with bas-reliefs on the pedestal, for his altar was completed, but the main *retablo* was left unfinished and was continued by his pupil,

PLATE XXVIII

SIMON OF CYRENE

From the *paso* of *Christ Bearing the Cross*
Valladolid. Museo Provincial de Bellas Artes

Luis de Llamosa. These works, also, have
been destroyed.

A fragment of an undated *retablo* from
the Monastery of *Carmelitas Descalzos,*
Valladolid, now in the *Museo Provincial,*
is a panel representing the Baptism of
Christ (Plate XXIV). As is customary
with Fernández, it is not so much a relief
as a composition of two figures attached
to a flat background on which is painted
a river, with clouds, cherubs' heads, the
Dove of the Holy Spirit, and the bust of
God the Father in low relief on the upper
portion. The figures are life-size, Christ
kneeling at the left, partially wrapped in
a cloak, while Saint John, standing at the
right, holds above His head a shell. The
saint is clad in a coarse garment which
leaves his left shoulder and his legs ex-
posed. A heavy cloak falling from his
right shoulder is gathered in his left hand.
Fernández shows a certain grasp of characterization in his contrasting of the
nervous leanness of the Baptist with the
smoother contours of Christ's form. In

*The Baptism
of Christ*

Saint John's head, too, there is a trace of the prophet's fire. The folds of the cloak about Christ's form are so broken and complicated that they distract the attention from the figure itself, which expresses in its slightly bowed head and folded arms the sacredness of the ceremony. One is seized with a desire to brush away the spiral clouds and merry little cherubs who clutter the background.

Retablo of the parish church, Cegama

Various other undated *retablos* ascribed to Fernández are those of the parish churches of Cegama and Nava del Rey, and of the Convent of *Agustinos Calzados* of Salamanca, the last-mentioned not extant. In the central relief of the Cegama *retablo* (Plate XXV) Saint Martin, like King Philip going a-hunting, a plume in his hat, stays his merry course long enough to sever his cloak, blown out by the wind, that it may fall on the beggar at his feet. The beggar, instead of being properly placed in the panel, stands on the cornice of the story below. On either side are Saint John the Baptist and Saint

PLATE XXIX

SAINT VERONICA

From the *paso* of *Christ Bearing the Cross*
Valladolid. Museo Provincial de Bellas Artes

Joseph. Below them are Saint Peter and
Saint Paul, flanking the tabernacle. Four
panels representing the Annunciation, the
Visitation, the Nativity, and the Adoration of the Magi fill the outer panels.
The central space in the attic is allotted to
the Crucifix with the Virgin and Saint
John. At the left is Saint Francis, and
at the right, Saint Anthony of Padua. At
the bottom of the *retablo* are small reliefs
of the four evangelists. Corinthian
columns separate the niches, and above the
arches which frame the saints' statues are
broken, scrolled pediments. This *retablo*
is attributed to Fernández by the Count de
la Viñaza, and it is related that there was
associated with him the native sculptor,
Juan García de Verástegui, whose name
also appears in connection with the works
for the convent of Aránzazu. The sum-
mary modeling of the heads and the tu-
bular folds of the drapery as well as the
variations in the architecture lead to the
conclusion that the *retablo* should be assigned to the sculptor of Cegama, who

during his association with Fernández at Aránzazu may well have assimilated his style. A more definite basis for this assumption is a statement made by a son of Verástegui, who says of his father, " ' He made the *retablo* ' " (58). Such a remark need not be taken as applying to the sculpture, but since internal evidence discounts the attribution to Fernández, all indications point to the Cegamese as the author.

Retablo of the Church of las Isabelas, Oñate

A *retablo* in the Church of *las Isabelas* at Oñate (Plate XXVI), whose central figure is that of Saint Anne, standing, leading the Virgin by the hand, is listed by the Count de la Viñaza (59) as among Fernández's works. It seems merely to show his influence in a slight angularity of the draperies. The faces show no trace of the master's manner, nor is the frame of his type.

This series of *retablos*, groups, and single figures comprises Fernández's work for the permanent decoration of churches. In the choice of subject, the types of faces, the treatment of draperies, they show their author's close interrelation with the life about him, but another series, related in subject matter but distinct in treatment, is an even stronger proof of the representative character of his work. This group consists of the figures for the processions of Holy Week.

VI

Holy Week, for Catholic Spain, is a period of devout ceremony. Among the most famed events are the processions. Cathedrals, churches, and brotherhoods have their processional figures stored away during the year and brought forth on this one occasion. These figures compose groups representing scenes from the Passion of Christ, so that the whole series displays in vivid tableaux the story of the suffering and death of the Lord. They are mounted on scaffolds borne through the streets on men's shoulders or on wheels. Curtains hung from the edges of the platforms to the ground conceal the means of locomotion. Among the characters which people the scenes, in addition to the august objects of the cult, are Jews and executioners, soldiers and tormentors, all the rabble who with jeers and with revilings

persecuted the Saviour. The same human-
izing influences which in other countries
led to miracle plays and the actual drama-
tization of the story of the New Testament, in Spain culminated, as well, in
these groups, waiting only the breath of
life to awake and act their allotted parts.
"Religion in these countries", says Gallenga, "is an affair of the senses, and it
little matters whether it is through a play
or a *tableau vivant* that it reaches the
heart. . . To see, to touch, is for a
Spaniard to believe; and the impression,
while it lasts, is genuine" (60).

In each town the processions assumed a
character of their own. Sevilla was famed
for ostentation, since every brotherhood
aspired to outdo the other in the splendour
of its images, many of which are the work
of Montañés. Almost all are *imágenes de
vestir*, that is, puppets, whose heads,
hands, and feet alone are sculpture, the
rest being hidden under massive garments
of silk or velvet heavy with gold and
embroidery. Not only do processional

as seen by
Miguel de
Unamuno

images proper have their place in these functions, but also other effigies of the Virgin or the Saviour held in popular esteem.

Even in smaller towns the celebration attracted people from the outlying districts and assumed the importance of a great affair. Such an one, as remembered from his childhood in Bilbao, is described by Miguel de Unamuno:

"Now they are coming. They approached with a solemn and inspiring sound, throb, throb, throb! Some men clad in black, with dominos or something similar, issuing from the murky street, beating time on the ground with their staves. They were the men who carried the *bultos*. Before them went, also clad in black, another man, marching backward like the guard of a squad of convicts: this man, thump! gave a stroke with a gavel and stopped those with the *bultos*. Then there came forth from under each one of these a boy with his wine flask, and all the bearers drank to regain strength with

PLATE XXX

THE BAD ROBBER

Valladolid. Museo Provincial de Bellas Artes

which to bear their cross through these
streets of God. The *bultos, corcho!* The
bultos, they weighed a little bit, I tell
you! . . .

"The most famous personages among
the figures were, and in all probability still
are, Anachu, with one hand drawn back
and with the other mocking the Lord under
his very nose, and Fracagorri, he of the
red breeches.

"There came next the Lord praying in
the Garden of Olives, and in it figured a
real tree, not a make-believe one.

"For lack of an olive tree, one was
counterfeited by a laurel, from which hung
oranges, a device which gave a fine effect,
aivá! nothing less than an actual tree. . .

"In the garden were sleeping the
apostles, a few garments attached to heads.

"There came the Supper, and before
that group was aroused to life in us the
narrative of the Passion, of that Passion
which we heard read in the mass with
such deep feeling. For us that was indeed
a mystery!" (61).

Of an earlier type is the procession in
Valladolid witnessed in 1605 and described
by Pinheiro da Veiga in these terms:

" In these days of Holy Week, the first
[procession] comes from the Trinity, a
standard of black damask with two tassels,
which two members of the brotherhood
dressed in black carry . . . then a member of the brotherhood with a cross, which
they make of thin boards, hollow inside
and all gilded, and although very large,
they are very easy to carry, and two large
torches, one on each side. There followed
four hundred disciplinants in two files in
processional order. . . Behind them four
hundred members of the brotherhood, clad
in black buckram, with their torches of
four wicks, all in the same order; and in
the midst of them the first *paso*, because
in place of our painted banners, they bear
sculptured *pasos*, of appropriate height,
the finest and most beautiful that can be
imagined, because those of Valladolid are
the best there are in Castilla, for the pro-
portions of the bodies, beauty of the faces,

and ornamentation of the figures, since all is of the same material, of pasteboard and canvas, of which they are formed; and if anyone is clothed, cap or cloak outside, it is all of brocade or cloth, so that they look very well. This *paso* was the Prayer in the Garden, with the disciples and the angel. There followed four hundred more disciplinants in the same order, and some of them with a single rosette (which they call *abrojo* [thistle]) which lacerates their sides. . . Behind them followed one hundred and fifty members of the brotherhood, with tapers and black tunics; and the *paso* was of Our Lady at the foot of the Cross, with Christ Our Lord in her arms, and the Marys; behind was a corregidor or *alcalde de corte* to prevent disturbances. So that the procession was composed of fourteen hundred disciplinants and six hundred and fifty members of the brotherhood. . . As this is ending, another issues from *San Francisco* to the Palace by the *Platería* and Cantarranas. This one was almost twice the size of the

first, because it included two thousand disciplinants and over a thousand members of
the brotherhood, with tunics and tapers,
all in the same order, and with the same
arrangement and distribution, and the *pasos*
many and very beautiful, and they are
mounted on tables or tabernacles some as
large as ordinary houses, which the members of the brotherhood themselves carry;
and as the figures are of canvas and card-
board, they are very light; but I can state
that I did not see figures nor images more
perfect, even on our most renowned altars
in Portugal. The first *paso* was the Supper,
very perfect in every way. The second,
the Prayer in the Garden with the angel
in a tree, much to see and with many
soldiers, and the cutting off of Malco's
ear. The third, the *paso* of Saint Veronica.
The fourth, how He was crucified. The
fifth, the lance thrust from Longinus on
horseback. The sixth, the Descent from
the Cross, so life-like, that no other seemed
so good, with the gravity and melancholy
of the *Santos Velhos*. The seventh, Christ

PLATE XXXI

THE GOOD ROBBER
Valladolid. Museo Provincial de Bellas Artes

Our Lord in the arms of the Virgin, with which the procession came to an end, and it was more than three hours in passing (very quickly) the places where we were; and none of them has more merit " (62).

In the same fashion are described several more processions. A comparison of this account with later ones shows that these early figures were of less durable materials, but that the fame which they had already acquired would lead to the employment of sculptors of renown in the perpetuation of the series.

The penitential churches were the repositories of the passion figures which are supposed to have been done under the supervision of Fernández. In three of these (*las Angustias, la Cruz,* and *la Pasión*) Ceán Bermúdez estimated the number to be more than seventy. The unequal merit of the statues, the addition of new ones following the traditional style, and the replacing and repairing of broken specimens leave the proportion of Fernández's actual share in them small. Many of them are now housed in the museum. It is here that Fernández most clearly shows himself a man of the people, bred in their habits and tastes. Indeed these creations might well be a collection of Valladolid's less savoury characters, of that ilk with whom Gil Blas may have consorted during his sojourn in the town: executioners, their faces twisted in an evil leer, performing their task with a right good will, turbaned Jews with cruel lips, soldiers clad in the conventional corselets of pseudo-Roman armour, all the ugly throng made hideous by the play of evil passions.

Paso of *Christ Bearing the Cross*

Those formerly in the Church of *la Pasión* but now in the museum are cited in a document dated 1614. In this contract Gregorio Fernández undertakes to make various statues representing "' . . . Jesus the Nazarene with the cross on His shoulders, Simon of Cyrene helping Him to carry it, an executioner pulling the rope, an armed man, and Veronica '" (63). For this he was paid two thousand *reales*.

Simon of Cyrene (Plate XXVIII) and *Saint Veronica* (Plate XXIX) are the only two of the original components which can now be positively identified.

Simon of Cyrene has all the vigour which creative genius, loosed in a new field untrammeled by convention, could give it. Clad in a wide-collared smock reaching to the knees, hood, and high boots, he resembles some uncouth countryman who has wandered from his flocks and upland pastures to be drawn into the surging mob, made to play an unwilling part in the great drama of which he would have preferred to be a spectator. The firm set of his feet as he strides forward, the strength of his sturdy shoulders leaning backward under the weight of the cross gripped in his arms, his muscular hands, all confirm the rugged power of his weatherbeaten face, half lost in the profusion of its beard. The swing of his body is balanced by the forward bend of the head.

Saint Veronica is leaning slightly forward gazing down at her hands, which should hold the handkerchief bearing the image of Christ. Her cloak falls from her shoulders, and a corner of it crosses her left knee. She is in a semi-crouching position. Her face, lost in swathing folds of wimple and head-covering, is very narrow at the chin; the lower lip is full, and the eyes are set close together.

Other *pasos* from *la Pasión*

In 1661 instructions for mounting the *pasos* list five groups in this church, two of which are designated as "new" and probably posterior to the time of Fernández. The others, in addition to that already mentioned, are the *paso* of *The Raising of the Cross,* and the *paso* of *The Humility of Christ Our Lord.* The characters of the former were:

"'Executioner who helps to raise the cross with the lance. . . — executioner who holds the ladder . . . — bad robber. . . — good robber . . . — young executioner who pulls the other rope . . . — executioner who supports the cross with his shoulder . . .'" (64).

PLATE XXXII

SAINT JOHN THE EVANGELIST
Valladolid. Church of las Angustias

It is interesting to note, and the fact
may be significant, that Francisco del
Rincón, the supposed teacher of Fernández, in the year 1604 also made some processional figures for this same church.
Perhaps it was in such commissions that
Fernández served his apprenticeship.
These figures are probably those listed in
the 1916 catalogue of the museum as
numbers 126, 132, 151, 150, 130 or 131,
and 133. They vary from Fernández's
usual style and might well be the work
of Rincón.

In the Church of *Jesús Nazareno,* in-
ventory of 1763, there were listed the
following processional figures of the school
of Fernández:

Pasos of the
Church of
*Jesús
Nazareno*

"'*Paso* of Christ Crucified. — has the
following figures: man playing at dice. —
figure with a wound in the head. — figure
with the kettle. — figure with the ladder. —
figure with the sponge.

"'*Paso* of Christ Despoiled. — has the
following figures: he who pulls the rope
and has a sword with a bar across it. —

figure who drills. — figure with the pick ' " (65).

These personages are now housed in the *Museo Provincial* and can be identified as numbers 136 through 139, omitting the " figure with the ladder ", and 127 through 129 of the 1916 catalogue.

Akin to the processional statues and probably belonging to the same class are the figures of the two robbers on their crosses which come from the Church of *las Angustias*. These works have been attributed to Pompeo Leoni but are more closely allied to Fernández's work. In the modeling of the bodies the fullness of the forms might suggest Leoni. The treatment of the heads bespeaks a closer affinity to the work of Fernández in the roundness of the eyeball, the sharply cut lines about the eyes, and the type of nose and mouth. The hair is treated more simply, in less detail than is usual. In the stiff, broken folds of the loin cloths his manner is well exemplified. Gestas, the bad robber (Plate XXX), his eyes glaring, his tongue protruding from swollen lips, has the muscles of his torso contracted as if he were endeavouring to tear himself from the cross. Dimas, the good robber (Plate XXXI), is quieter. His head, the eyes closed, is sunk forward. His body hangs limply without a struggle. It is not probable that Leoni would have been concerned in a work of minor importance so far removed from the sphere of his usual activities, aside from the slight artistic relation it bears to his works.

Remaining in the Church of *las Angustias* and attributed to Fernández are a *Saint John* (Plate XXXII) and a *Saint Mary Magdalene* (Plate XXXIII). The Magdalene, her hair loose on her shoulders, is distracted in her grief. A cloak is wound about her form, the attitude being a reversal of that of *Saint Veronica* of the *paso* of *Christ Bearing the Cross*. The folds of her gown above the waist are like those of *Saint Veronica*. Saint John's cloak is cast loosely over his right shoulder. His hands are slightly extended

Saint John and Saint Mary Magdalene

and his face upturned. There is a certain muscularity in the throats and faces, a softness and freedom in the folds, especially those of Saint John's cloak which are unusual with Fernández, but which may be referable to the greater spontaneity noticeable in all the processional figures.

A more imposing assemblage than any of these is *The Descent from the Cross* in the Church of *la Cruz* (Plate **XXXIV**). This machine, because of its great weight, was called *el Reventón* and was carried on wheels instead of on men's shoulders. Nicodemus and Joseph of Arimathea, clad in full-skirted coats and turbans, have mounted upon ladders and are detaching the body of the Saviour from the cross. Saint John stands below at the right, ready to receive the Lord's body. A man behind the ladder is pulling the nails from Christ's feet. The Magdalene, at the left, gazes up at Him, but one hand motions towards the Holy Mother as if to point out where Christ's body should rest. The Virgin herself is seated on a rock, her arms out-

PLATE XXXIII

SAINT MARY MAGDALENE
Valladolid.   Church of las Angustias

stretched, awaiting her sad burden. Although the sculptor completed this group, he died before receiving his pay for it. When his widow made her will in 1661, she declared that the brotherhood still owed about a thousand *ducados* for the work. She stated that a law suit had been instituted and that when it came to appraising the work the brotherhood had hidden the group and refused to produce it, so that the suit could not be settled. In 1667 it was still being carried on by Fernández's son-in-law.

In all these groups of figures the artistic element is entirely subordinated to the pictorial. They were made as nearly lifelike as possible without regard for other considerations. Their interest lies in their relation to the rest of the sculptor's work, showing as they do his intimate connection with the taste for realism which characterized his public. The story was the thing, and if some sculptural effect was achieved by the way, it was a secondary consideration.

VII

With Fernández's death the importance
of Valladolid as a centre of artistic effort
waned. He must have had many sculptors employed in his studio who probably
continued to work in his style. The few
names of assistants which are mentioned in
documents here and there are otherwise unknown, nor are they identified with works
of their own which would give them distinct artistic personalities. Even though he
left no pupils of merit in Valladolid, his
influence can be traced over a wide area.
Not only is his own work scattered through
the Basque countries, but that it had followers there is attested by the *retablo* of
las Isabelas at Oñate. If the conclusions
which would make Juan García de Verástegui responsible for the *retablo* of
Cegama are correct, his close affiliation
with the style of Fernández would mark

him as one of his adherents. Luis Fernández de la Vega, who worked in Gijón and Oviedo, appropriated the surface characteristics of his supposed master and diffused them in the Asturias. In Salamanca, too, several *retablos* bore witness to the popularity of his manner.

Aside from these sporadic outgrowths, the main effect of his work made itself felt in central Spain, where was gathered a group of sculptors second only to that in Andalucía. To Madrid, in the train of courtier and parasite, flocked the artists. Here were Manuel Pereira, the Portuguese, whom tradition supposes to have received his training in Valladolid, and his pupils Manuel Gutiérrez and Manuel Delgado. Here, too, was Pedro Alonso de los Ríos, who, born in Valladolid after Fernández's death, worked in Madrid and had a number of disciples. As late as the eighteenth century Luis Salvador Carmona, deriving from the school of Los Ríos, carried on the tradition, though in a spirit more allied to that of the Sevillian school. It is impos-

School of
Madrid

sible to trace any personal relation between this new group and the Valladolid master, but their artistic kinship is evident. There are in Madrid several statues by Fernández which may have served as models for later sculptors. The *Cristo del Pardo*, the *Saint Augustine* and *Saint Monica* of the Church of *la Encarnación* are typical of his treatment of such figures. The first, in particular, was repeatedly copied. These men followed the general trend of purely national inspiration which he had marked out. His manner of treating draperies in broad planes, the attitudes which he had used were adopted. Eagerly espousing his realistic methods, but without his sobriety, his successors debased them for theatrical effects. Approaching their subjects with less reverence, they lost the accent of other-worldliness which redeems Fernández's sculpture from the commonplace. The unfortunate expedient of introducing eyes made of crystal in later times resulted in the clothing of statues in garments of real cloth and in the addition of eyelashes

PLATE XXXIV

PASO OF THE DESCENT FROM THE CROSS
Valladolid. Church of la Cruz

and coiffures of actual hair. Nor did his own work escape the ravages of the trend he had started, as witness the mutilation of the *Cristo del Conjo*.

Fernández cannot claim the entire artistic parentage of the group which grew up in the "only Court". It drew also, to a less degree, from his great Sevillian contemporary, Juan Martínez Montañés. They were both nationalists, both realists, but their modes of working were very different, and their temperaments as distinct as the provinces which claimed them: in Fernández an earnest intensity in harmony with the uncompromising Castilian plains; in Montañés a sweet prodigality which marks him as Murillo's brother spirit. Where Fernández's chief preoccupation was the suffering Christ, the sorrowing Mother, the Sevillian preferred to depict Our Lady in virgin beauty, or saints in devout meditation, unmarred by too painful penitence. Methods as well as subjects further emphasize these differences. In Montañés's modeling the forms are softer and rounder;

Comparison with Montañés

the harshness and dryness which occasionally disfigure Fernández's work are absent,
but, in exchange, there is less directness,
less power. Where the Castilian's draperies
are broad and stiff, the Sevillian's are
voluminous, with heavy, soft folds. How
the two currents met and combined is illustrated by the fact that Mena, bred in
the Sevillian school, yet used Fernández's
Magdalene as a model.

Close upon the precedents of these two
came a wave of baroque influences from
Bernini in Italy which culminated in such
monuments as the monstrous *Transparente*
of Toledo Cathedral. Although Fernández
exhibited sporadic symptoms of that
fashion in his use of unsculptural subjects,
responsibility for the movement can hardly
be laid at his door. The treatment of
draperies, the hysteria of the figures, all
the theatrical apparatus of these products
point to an immediate derivation from
Italy.

The immense vogue of Fernández's work
proves that he did strike a chord of national

sympathy. The range of emotions in which he dealt, true to his Spanish lineage, was small. The agony of the Passion, visualized in a more sober and serene key than that of his forerunners, and the ecstasies of saints attracted his hand. Gentler subjects such as the intimate and tender aspects of the Virgin and Child dear to the heart of a Della Robbia were as foreign to him as the brooding titans of a Michael Angelo. Passion for reality combined with simplicity of method and restraint of expression, all subordinated to an intense religious feeling, give him his individual character. His sincerity made him a faithful exponent of the religious ideals of the Spain which he knew. His devout spirit cast a momentary spell upon the troubled waters of Spanish art.

NOTES

(1) The form of name used in the artist's signature has been adopted, although contemporary documents use both forms, Fernández and Hernández, indiscriminately.

(2) Pardo Bazán, Emilia, *condesa* de. *Por la España pintoresca*. Barcelona [1895?]. p. 112-113, *tr.*

(3) Cock, Enrique. *Jornada de Tarazona hecha por Felipe II en 1592*. Madrid, 1879. p. 25-26, *tr.*

(4) Pinheiro da Veiga, Tomé. *La fastiginia* in Sociedad castellana de excursiones. *Boletín*. March 1915. v. 7, p. 56, *tr.*

(5) Ceán Bermúdez, J. A. *Diccionario histórico de los más ilustres profesores de las bellas artes en España*. Madrid, 1800. v. 2, p. 263.

(6) Martí y Monsó, José. *Gregorio Fernández, su vida y sus obras* in *Museum*. 1912. v. 2, p. 214-215.

(7) —— *Estudios histórico-artísticos relativos principalmente á Valladolid*. Valladolid-Madrid [1898-1901]. p. 406-407.

(8) —— *Gregorio Fernández* in *Museum*. 1912. v. 2, p. 217.

(9) —— *Estudios histórico-artísticos.* p. 401, *tr.*

(10) —— —— p. 418, *tr.*

(11) Pinheiro da Veiga, in Sociedad castellana de excursiones. *Boletín.* August 1913. v. 6, p. 192, *tr.*

(12) Martí y Monsó. *Estudios histórico-artísticos.* p. 422.

(13) Bosarte, Isidoro. *Viage artístico á varios pueblos de España.* Madrid, 1804. p. 196–197, *tr.*

(14) Sobremonte, Matías de. *Historia del convento de San Francisco, de Valladolid,* quoted in Martí y Monsó, José. *Nuevas noticias de arte extraídas y comentadas de un libro hasta hace poco inédito* in Sociedad castellana de excursiones. *Boletín.* January 1905. v. 2, p. 4.

(15) Martí y Monsó. *Estudios histórico-artísticos.* p. 400, *tr.*

(16) *Idem, tr.*

(17) *Idem, tr.*

(18) *Idem, tr.*

(19) Martí y Monsó. *Estudios histórico-artísticos.* p. 399, *tr.*

(20) Viñaza, Cipriano Muñoz y Manzano, *conde* de la. *Adiciones al diccionario histórico . . . de D. Juan Agustín Ceán Bermúdez.* Madrid, 1889–94. v. 2, p. 255, *tr.*

(21) —— —— v. 2, p. 257, *tr.*

AND MONOGRAPHS

(22) Martí y Monsó. *Estudios histórico-artísticos.* p. 410, *tr.*

(23) —— —— p. 400–401, *tr.*

(24) Llaguno y Amírola, Eugenio. *Noticias de los arquitectos y arquitectura de España desde su restauración.* Madrid, 1829. v. 3, p. 178.

(25) —— —— v. 3, p. 184–185.

(26) Agapito y Revilla, Juan. *Valladolid: Un retablo conocido y unas esculturas no vulgarizadas* in Sociedad castellana de excursiones. *Boletín.* July 1913. v. 6, p. 148.

(27) —— —— p. [145]–150.

(28) The term *estofado* is used to indicate that method of polychromy in which rich brocades were imitated by the use of gold underlying all the other colours and appearing in patterns where they were scratched away.

(29) Rivadeneira, Pedro de. *Flos sanctorvm.* Madrid, 1599–1601. v. 2, p. 209, *tr.*

(30) Agapito y Revilla. *Arquitectura de los antiguos retablos de Valladolid* in *Arquitectura y construcción.* Barcelona, 1918. p. 44.

(31) —— *Los retablos de Medina del Campo* in Sociedad castellana de excursiones. *Boletín.* February 1916. v. 7, p. 320.

(32) Ponz, Antonio. *Viage fuera de España.* Madrid, 1785. v. 1, p. 22.

(33) Bosarte. p. 202.

(34) Martí y Monsó. *Estudios histórico-artísticos*. p. 398, *tr.*

(35) Dieulafoy, M. A. *La statuaire poly-chrome en Espagne*. Paris, 1908. p. 139, *tr.*

(36) Bosarte. p. 200–201.

(37) Sangrador Vitores, Matías. *Historia de la muy noble y leal ciudad de Valladolid*. Valladolid, 1851–54. v. 2, p. 218–219.

(38) Dieulafoy. p. 139–140, *tr.*

(39) Serrano Fatigati, Enrique. *Escultura en Madrid*. Madrid, 1912. p. 31.

(40) Sobremonte, quoted in Agapito y Revilla. *Valladolid: Un retablo conocido y unas esculturas no vulgarizadas* in Sociedad castellana de excursiones. *Boletín*. August 1913. v. 6, p. 173–175.

(41) Viñaza, *conde* de la. v. 2, p. 260.

(42) Bosarte. p. 339–340.

(43) Tormo y Monzó, Elías. *Mis mañanitas valisoletanas: Tras de Becerra, y Goya al paso* in Sociedad castellana de excursiones. *Boletín*. October 1912. v. 5, p. 520.

(44) Agapito y Revilla. *Tradiciones de Valladolid* in Sociedad castellana de excursiones. *Boletín*. April 1914. v. 6, p. 365–366.

(45) Martí y Monsó. *Estudios histórico-artísticos*. p. 401.

(46) Tr. by Thomas Walsh in his *Hispanic anthology*. New York, 1920. p. 261–262.

(47) Mesonero Romanos, Manuel. *El arte en las iglesias de Madrid* in *La Ilustración*

española y americana. January 8th, 1902. año XLVI, p. 13.

(48) Serrada, Bernardo la. *Recopilación de la vida, excelencias y gracias de la gloriosa Santa Ana,* quoted in Viñaza, *conde* de la. v. 2, p. 260–262.

(49) Martí y Monsó. *Estudios histórico-artísticos.* p. 399, note 1, *tr.*

(50) Viñaza, *conde* de la. v. 2, p. 255, *tr.*

(51) *Idem, tr.*

(52) Ceán Bermúdez. v. 2, p. 267.

(53) Bosarte. p. 208.

(54) The Carmelite monk to whom this incident refers was an English recluse, an early general of the order, the founder of the Brotherhood of the Scapulary under the guidance of the Virgin, who appeared to him in a vision. The members of the brotherhood were to wear a small scapulary in commemoration of this sacred event.

(55) Rivadeneira. Madrid, 1675. pt. 3. p. 679–678 [*i.e.* 680], *tr.*

(56) Benavides, José. *Nota que facilita D. José Benavides, chantre de la catedral de Plasencia, a los señores de la Sociedad española de excursiones, que visitan los principales monumentos de esta ciudad, hoy 6 de enero de 1905* in Sociedad española de excursiones. *Boletín.* February 1905. año XIII, p. 41–42.

(57) Agapito y Revilla. *Los retablos de*

Medina del Campo in Sociedad castellana de excursiones. *Boletín.* February 1916. v. 7, p. 320.

(58) Copied from a printed notice by T. Larrea in the sacristy of the church.

(59) Viñaza, *conde* de la. v. 2, p. 260.

(60) Gallenga, A. C. N. *Iberian reminiscences.* London, 1883. v. 1, p. 241–242.

(61) Unamuno y Jugo, Miguel de. *De mi país.* Madrid, 1903. p. 78–79, *tr.*

(62) Pinheiro da Veiga, in Sociedad castellana de excursiones. *Boletín.* April 1913. v. 6, p. 78–79, *tr.*

(63) Martí y Monsó. *Estudios histórico-artísticos.* p. 499, *tr.*

(64) *Idem, tr.*

(65) Martí y Monsó. *Estudios histórico-artísticos.* p. 496, *tr.*

LIST OF WORKS

In this list are included those works whose authenticity is supported by documents and those whose artistic character warrants their acceptance.

ARÁNZAZU
  SANTUARIO DE NUESTRA SEÑORA DE ARÁNZAZU
  Retablo mayor and collaterals (not extant). See p. 109–110.

AVILA
  CONVENTO DE SANTA TERESA
  Saint Theresa. See p. 96–97, Plate XXII.

EIBAR
  CONVENTO DE FRANCISCAS
  Retablo mayor and collaterals. See p. 88–93, Plate XIX.

MADRID
  CONVENTO DE CAPUCHINOS DEL PARDO
  Cristo del Pardo. See p. 80–82, Plate XII.
  CONVENTO DE LA ENCARNACIÓN
  Saint Augustine. See p. 82–83, Plate XV.
  Saint Monica. See p. 82–83, Plate XIV.
  IGLESIA DE SAN PLÁCIDO
  Cristo Yacente. See p. 81–82, Plate XIII.
  MUSEO DEL PRADO
  Cristo Yacente. See p. 82.

LIST OF WORKS OF DOUBTFUL AUTHENTICITY

In this list are included those works which, although attributed to Fernández, seem rather to be copies or by his pupils and followers.

ALCALÁ DE HENARES
  ORATORIO DE SAN FELIPE NERI
    Saint Theresa
      Although noted as authentic by Tormo y Monzó (*Cartillas excursionistas "Tormo": Alcalá de Henares.* p. 148), this figure seems to be a copy of the *Saint Theresa* in the *Museo Provincial*, Valladolid. The modeling of the face is too harsh to be ascribed to Fernández.

AVILA
  CONVENTO DE SANTA TERESA
    Christ at the Column
      Listed as authentic by Ceán Bermúdez (v. 2, p. 569), Ponz (v. 12, p. 320), Dieulafoy (*La statuaire polychrome.* p. 139), and Tormo y Monzó (*Cartillas excursionistas "Tormo": Avila.* p. 214), but varying from Fernández's typical work. See p. 77.

CONJO
  PARROQUIA
    Cristo del Conjo

Cited as authentic by Ceán Bermúdez
(v. 2, p. 271), Díaz (p. 206-207), and
Núñez (p. [337]-338).

MADRID
CONVENTO DE BERNARDAS DEL SACRAMENTO
Cristo Yacente
Noted by Tormo y Monzó (*Visitando lo
no-visitable: La clausura de las Bernardas
del Sacramento.* p. 127). It repeats Fernández's type but differs radically in the
modeling of the head.

CONVENTO DE LA ENCARNACIÓN
Christ at the Column
Noted by Luis Muñoz (p. 236) as by
Fernández and accepted by Orueta (*Gregorio Hernández.* p. 48) but not by Tormo
y Monzó (*Visitando lo no-visitable: Apéndice a la visita a la clausura de la Encarnación.* p. 181). This figure is even more
slender than the one in the Church of
la Cruz, Valladolid, and the weak outlines
of the face mark it as a school work.
Cristo Yacente
Noted by Luis Muñoz (p. 239) and accepted by Orueta (*Gregorio Hernández.*
p. 47-48) and Tormo y Monzó (*Visitando
lo no-visitable: La clausura de la Encarnación de Madrid.* p. 126). The eyeballs,
upturned so that only the lower edges of
the pupils are visible, the disheveled hair,
and sunken jaw accentuate the more
gruesome aspects of the scene. This example seems certainly not by Fernández.

The Immaculate Conception

Cited by Luis Muñoz (p. 237) and accepted by Orueta (*Gregorio Hernández.* p. 32–34) and Tormo y Monzó (*Visitando lo no-visitable: La clausura de la Encarnación de Madrid.* p. 127). It seems to be a poor copy based on the model which Fernández popularized. The face has lost its pure outlines and clear-cut features, the mouth shrinking to a smaller compass than that of the eyes. The hair is spread on the shoulders in set array, while two locks straggle over the bulbous forehead. This figure is a sad precursor of the *imágenes de vestir* which were to follow. It is merely a representation of heavy garments from which protrude a head and hands having no apparent connection with a body underneath.

PONTEVEDRA

IGLESIA DE SAN BARTOLOMÉ

The Repentant Magdalene

Rejected by Murguía (p. 728) but tentatively accepted by Orueta (*La vida y la obra de Pedro de Mena y Medrano.* p. 177–178). Greatly inferior to *The Repentant Magdalene* of the Church of *San Miguel,* Valladolid, it is probably either a copy or a school work.

VALLADOLID

CONVENTO DE SAN DIEGO DE DESCALZOS FRANCISCOS

The Immaculate Conception

This image, in the present *retablo mayor,* corresponds to the type created by Fernández. The sculpture of the original *retablo* has been removed to the *Museo Provincial*, and the origin of this statue is unknown. Not only does it repeat, with slight variations, Fernández's type of figure, but also the pedestal bears a lozenge and bar decoration, a characteristic feature of his work.

CONVENTO DE SAN PABLO
Cristo Yacente
Listed by Ponz (v. 11, p. 59) as attributed to Fernández. Although the design is the same as that of the *Cristo del Pardo*, neither the modeling nor the folds resemble Fernández's work.

IGLESIA DE SAN MIGUEL (present church)
Saint Peter, Saint Paul, Saint James the Great, Saint Philip, Cardinal Virtues from the *retablo mayor*. See p. 43–47, Plate I.

IGLESIA PENITENCIAL DE LA CRUZ
Ecce Homo
Listed in Ponz (v. 11, p. 56) and Sangrador Vitores (v. 2, p. 218–219). The stiff poise of the body with its rigid forearm, the casual rendering of the face place this figure below the level of Fernández's personal work.

MUSEO PROVINCIAL DE BELLAS ARTES
Saint Mary Magdalene. See p. 70.
Saint Sebastian. See p. 86.
Los Cuatro Durmientes (processional figures from the Church of *las Angustias*)
The modeling of the faces allies them with authentic works.

Executioner Throwing Dice (processional figure from the *paso* of *Christ Crucified* of the Church of *Jesús Nazareno*). Catalogue no. 136. See p. 123.

El Descalabrado (processional figure from the *paso* of *Christ Crucified* of the Church of *Jesús Nazareno*). Catalogue no. 137. See p. 123.

Soldier with a Kettle (processional figure from the *paso* of *Christ Crucified* of the Church of *Jesús Nazareno*). Catalogue no. 138. See p. 123.

Executioner who Raises the Sponge (processional figure from the *paso* of *Christ Crucified* of the Church of *Jesús Nazareno*). Catalogue no. 139. See p. 123.

Executioner Pulling the Rope (processional figure from the *paso* of *Christ Despoiled* of the Church of *Jesús Nazareno*). Catalogue no. 127. See p. 123.

Executioner who Drills (processional figure from the *paso* of *Christ Despoiled* of the Church of *Jesús Nazareno*). Catalogue no. 128. See p. 123–124.

Executioner with a Pickax (processional figure from the *paso* of *Christ Despoiled* of the Church of *Jesús Nazareno*). Catalogue no. 129. See p. 123–124.

Executioner with a Lance (processional figure from the *paso* of *The Raising of the Cross* of the Church of *la Pasión*). Possibly catalogue no. 126. See p. 122.

Executioner who Holds the Ladder (processional figure from the *paso* of *The Raising*

of the Cross of the Church of *la Pasión*).
  Probably catalogue no. 132. See p. 122.
Bad Robber before Crucifixion (processional
  figure from the *paso* of *The Raising of the
  Cross* of the Church of *la Pasión*). Prob-
  ably catalogue no. 151. See p. 122.
Good Robber before Crucifixion (processional
  figure from the *paso* of *The Raising of the
  Cross* of the Church of *la Pasión*). Prob-
  ably catalogue no. 150. See p. 122.
Young Executioner who Pulls the Other Rope
  (processional figure from the *paso* of *The
  Raising of the Cross* of the Church of *la
  Pasión*). Probably catalogue no. 130 or
  131. See p. 122.
*Executioner who Supports the Cross with his
  Shoulder* (processional figure from the
  paso of *The Raising of the Cross* of the
  Church of *la Pasión*). Probably cata-
  logue no. 133. See p. 122.

VERGARA
  SEMINARIO
    Saint Ignatius of Loyola
      Cited as authentic by Ceán Bermúdez (v.
      2, p. 270) and Orueta (*Gregorio Hernández.*
      p. 38–40). See p. 85, Plate XVII.

VITORIA
  IGLESIA DE SAN PEDRO
    Mater Dolorosa
      Attributed to Fernández by Colá y Goiti
      (p. 50), Becerro de Bengoa (p. 158–159),
      and Valverde y Alvarez (p. 782). See
      p. 93–95, Plate XX.

In addition to the above list there are various
works bearing little or no relation to Fernández's
sculpture which have been ascribed to him. The
Pietà of the Carmelite convent at Burgos, the
retablo of *las Isabelas* at Oñate, and the *retablo*
of the parish church of Cegama have been dis-
cussed in the text. The soft, restrained folds of
the *Saint Francis* in the *Museo Provincial* at
Valladolid justify the conclusion reached in the
1916 catalogue that it is not by Fernández. Various figures from the old *retablo* of the Convent
of *San Diego*, now in the *Museo Provincial*,
although attributed to Fernández by Ceán Bermúdez and Ponz, are now known to have been
commissioned to Pompeo Leoni and probably
executed from his sketches. Other statues in
the museum occasionally but erroneously attributed to Fernández are the *Saint Elizabeth* (also
called *Saint Anne*) now ascribed to Juní, the
Saint Bruno now ascribed to Pedro Alonso de los
Ríos, the *Saint Peter* now attributed to Esteban
Jordán, and a *Saint Liberata*, a *Saint Monica*, and
a *Saint Scholastica* by unknown authors. *Cristos Yacentes* in the Monasteries of *Santa Ana* and
Santa Catalina, Valladolid, are poor repetitions
of the familiar type. An *Immaculate Conception*
in the Church of *San Esteban*, Salamanca,
although considered authentic by Agapito y
Revilla and Tormo y Monzó and slightly related
to Fernández's in posture, is entirely different
in type of face and treatment of draperies. If
the *retablo* now in the Church of *San Esteban*,
Valladolid, is the one taken from the Convent
of the *Carmen Calzado* in Medina del Campo,
attributed to Fernández, it bears no mark of his
handiwork.

LIST OF WORKS CITED

This list is made up of those works mentioned by various authors of which no reproductions are available. Although many of them are cited with small assurance, the impossibility of determining their merit warrants their inclusion.

LAGUNA DE DUERO
  PARROQUIA
    Cristo de los Trabajos
      Tentatively attributed by Martí y Monsó (*Estudios*. p. 401).

MADRID
  REAL CONVENTO DE PADRES CARMELITAS
    Saint Anne. See p. 83–84.

MEDINA DE RIOSECO
  CONVENTO DE CARMELITOS DESCALZOS
    Virgen del Carmen
      Cited by Ceán Bermúdez (v. 2, p. 268–269) as a repetition of that formerly in the Convent of *Carmelitas Calzados*, Valladolid.

NAVA DEL REY
  PARROQUIA
    Retablo mayor
      Listed as authentic by Ceán Bermúdez (v. 2, p. 269) and Ponz (v. 12, p. 170–171).

SAHAGÚN
  MONASTERIO DE BENEDICTINOS
    Retablo mayor and *retablo* of *San Benito*

Listed as authentic by Ceán Bermúdez
(v. 2, p. 268), Ponz (v. 11, p. 207), and
others; not extant.

SAN CEBRIÁN DE CAMPOS
PARROQUIA
Jesus the Nazarene
Cited in Ceán Bermúdez (v. 2, p. 268).

SANTIAGO DE COMPOSTELA
IGLESIA DE JESÚS
Saint Francis Xavier and *Saint Ignatius of
Loyola*
Cited by Ceán Bermúdez (v. 2, p. 271),
Murguía (p. 558–559), and Díaz (p. 206–
207).

SEGOVIA
CATEDRAL
Cristo Yacente
Cited by Tormo y Monzó (*Cartillas ex-
cursionistas "Tormo": Segovia.* p. 133).
IGLESIA DE SAN MARTÍN
Cristo Yacente
Cited by Tormo y Monzó (*Cartillas ex-
cursionistas "Tormo": Segovia.* p. 206).

TRUJILLO
PARROQUIA DE SANTIAGO
Saint James the Great
Cited by Ceán Bermúdez (v. 2, p. 270)
and Ponz (v. 7, p. 169).

TUDELA DE DUERO
PARROQUIA
Virgen del Rosario
Cited by Ceán Bermúdez (v. 2, p. 269)
and Ponz (v. 11, p. 19).

VALLADOLID

CONVENTO DE CARMELITAS DESCALZOS

Virgen del Carmen
Reputed by Sangrador Vitores (v. 2, p. 280) to be a repetition of that formerly in the Convent of the *Carmen Calzado*, Valladolid.

CONVENTO DE SAN PABLO

Mortuary statue of a knight in armour
Cited by the Count de la Viñaza (v. 2, p. 260) and by Bosarte (p. 210, 226).

IGLESIA DE SAN LORENZO

Virgen de la Candelaria
Cited by Ceán Bermúdez (v. 2, p. 267), Sangrador Vitores (v. 2, p. 201), Bosarte (p. 210), and Ponz (v. 11, p. 88) as a repetition of the one in the Church of *la Cruz*, Valladolid.

Virgen del Carmen
Cited by Ortega y Rubio (v. 2, p. 264).

IGLESIA DE SAN MIGUEL (present church)

Saint Anthony of Padua
Noted as attributed to Fernández by Agapito y Revilla (*Valladolid: Un retablo conocido.* p. 146).

Saint Francis Borgia
Cited by Bosarte (p. 210–211), Sangrador Vitores (v. 2, p. 271), and Ceán Bermúdez (v. 2, p. 267), and by Agapito y Revilla (*Valladolid: Un retablo conocido.* p. 146) as not extant.

IGLESIA DE SAN NICOLÁS

Ecce homo
Cited by Sangrador Vitores (v. 2, p. 291)

AND MONOGRAPHS

as attributed to Fernández and by Madoz
(v. 15, p. 559).
Christ at the Column
Cited by Martí y Monsó (*Gregorio Fernán-
dez.* p. 236) as attributed to Fernández.
IGLESIA DE SANTIAGO
Saint James the Great
Cited by Ortega y Rubio (v. 2, p. 264) and
Madoz (v. 15, p. 557) as attributed to
Fernández.
IGLESIA PENITENCIAL DE JESÚS NAZARENO
Jesus the Nazarene
Attributed to Fernández by Sangrador
Vitores (v. 2, p. 221–222) and Madoz (v.
15, p. 560).
IGLESIA PENITENCIAL DE LA CRUZ
The Prayer in the Garden (paso)
Cited by Ponz (v. 11, p. 56), Sangrador
Vitores (v. 2, p. 218–219), and Madoz
(v. 15, p. 560).
Virgen de la Candelaria
Cited by Ponz (v. 11, p. 56), Bosarte
(p. 210), and Sangrador Vitores (v. 2,
p. 218–219).
IGLESIA PENITENCIAL DE LA PASIÓN
Christ at the Column
Cited by Sangrador Vitores (v. 2, p. 210–
211).
The Prayer in the Garden
Cited by Sangrador Vitores (v. 2, p. 210–
211).

VITORIA
MONASTERIO DE NUESTRA SEÑORA DE LA CON-
CEPCIÓN DE DESCALZOS FRANCISCOS

Saint Anthony and *Saint Francis* on the
façade
Listed as attributed to Fernández by
Ceán Bermúdez (v. 2, p. 270) and without question by Madoz (v. 16, p. 345);
not extant?

ZAMORA
  CARMELITAS
    Saint Theresa
      Cited by Ceán Bermúdez (v. 2, p. 269).

BIBLIOGRAPHY

AGAPITO Y REVILLA, Juan. *Arquitectura de los antiguos retablos de Valladolid* in *Arquitectura y construcción*. Barcelona, 1918. p. 29–45.

—— *Del Valladolid monumental: La iglesia del convento de San Pablo* in Sociedad castellana de excursiones. *Boletín.* September 1911. v. 5, p. 195; October 1911. v. 5, p. 209, 213, 216.

—— *La obra de los maestros de la escultura vallisoletana: Papeletas razonadas para un catálogo* in *Castilla artística é histórica.* January 1917. v. 1, p. 9–10; February 1917. v. 1, p. 38–40.

—— *Reseña bibliográfica: Tres libros interesantes* in Sociedad castellana de excursiones. *Boletín.* March 1914. v. 6, p. 358–359.

—— *Los retablos de Medina del Campo* in Sociedad castellana de excursiones. *Boletín.* February 1916. v. 7, p. 314–322; March 1916. v. 7, p. 347–349; May 1916. v. 7, p. 392–395.

—— *Tradiciones de Valladolid* in Sociedad castellana de excursiones. *Boletín.* April 1914. v. 6, p. 365–366, 367.

—— *Valladolid: Los retablos de San Benito el Real* in Sociedad castellana de excursiones. *Boletín.* October 1913. v. 6, p. 225–226.

—— *Valladolid: Un retablo conocido y unas esculturas no vulgarizadas* in Sociedad castellana de excursiones. *Boletín.* July 1913. v. 6, p. 146–153; August 1913. v. 6, p. 173–175.

ARAUJO Y GÓMEZ, Fernando de. *Historia de la escultura en España desde principios del siglo XVI hasta fines del XVIII y causas de su decadencia.* Madrid, 1885. p. 316–329.

ASENSIO, Jesús. *Visita al Museo provincial de bellas artes, al Arqueológico y Biblioteca de Santa Cruz* in Sociedad castellana de excursiones. *Boletín.* March 1904. v. 1, p. 234–236.

BECERRO DE BENGOA, Ricardo. *El libro de Alava.* Vitoria, 1877. p. 157–159.

BENAVIDES, José. *Nota que facilita D. José Benavides, chantre de la catedral de Plasencia, á los señores de la Sociedad española de excursiones, que visitan los principales monumentos de esta ciudad, hoy 6 de enero de 1905* in Sociedad española de excursiones. *Boletín.* February 1905. año XIII, p. 40–43.

BERTAUX, Emile. *La fin de la Renaissance en Espagne* in Michel, André. *Histoire de l'art depuis les premiers temps chrétiens jusqu'à nos jours.* Paris, 1913. v. 5, pt. 2, p. [793]–844.

BOSARTE, Isidoro. *Viage artístico á varios pueblos de España.* Madrid, 1804.

CALVERT, Albert Frederick. *Sculpture in Spain.* London, New York, 1912. p. 104–116.

CEÁN BERMÚDEZ, Juan Agustín. *Diccionario histórico de los más ilustres profesores de las bellas artes en España.* Madrid, 1800. 6 v.

CHICOTE, Darío. *Visitas y paseos por Valladolid: Las Huelgas y la Magdalena* in Sociedad castellana de excursiones. *Boletín.* November 1903. v. 1, p. 139, 140.

COLÁ Y GOITI, José. *La ciudad de Vitoria.* Vitoria, 1883. p. 37–38, 50, [63]–64.

Compendio histórico y descriptivo de Valladolid. Valladolid, 1843.

DÍAZ, Angel. *Una excursión artística á Compostela y á la exposición regional* in Sociedad castellana de excursiones. *Boletín.* August 1909. v. 4, p. 188–191; September 1909. v. 4, p. 205–207.

DIEULAFOY, Marcel Auguste. *Art in Spain and Portugal*. New York, 1913. p. 239–240, 242.
—— *La statuaire polychrome en Espagne*. Paris, 1908. p. 131–142.

DOMÍNGUEZ BARRUETE, Roque. *Visitas y paseos por Valladolid: La casa de Berruguete, iglesia de San Benito y parroquia de San Miguel y San Julián* in Sociedad castellana de excursiones. *Boletín*. December 1905. v. 2, p. 236.

FALCÓN Y OZCOIDI, Modesto. *Salamanca artística y monumental*. Salamanca, 1867. p. 98–99, 136–137.

FIGUEROA, *Marqués* de. *Impresiones de una excursión á Mérida, Cáceres y Plasencia* in Sociedad española de excursiones. *Boletín*. February 1905. año XIII, p. [21]-39.

FORD, Richard. *A handbook for travellers in Spain*. London, 1890. 2 v.

LAFOND, Paul. *Le musée de Valladolid* in *Les Arts*. July 1905. no. 43, p. 23–28, 30.
—— *La sculpture espagnole*. Paris [1908]. p. 186–187, 195–200, 208.

LLAGUNO Y AMÍROLA, Eugenio. *Noticias de los arquitectos y arquitectura de España desde su restauración*. Madrid, 1829. v. 3, p. 148, 178, 184–185.

AND MONOGRAPHS

LOGA, Valerian von. *Die Spanische Plastik* in Knapp, Friedrich. *Die Italienische Plastik vom XV. bis XVIII. Jahrhundert.* Berlin [n.d.]. p. 121–144.

MADOZ, Pascual. *Diccionario geográfico-estadístico-histórico de España.* Madrid, 1845–50. 16 v.

Manual del viagero en las provincias vascongadas. Madrid, 1847. p. 32–33, 69, 122.

Manual histórico y descriptivo de Valladolid. Valladolid, 1861.

MARTÍ Y MONSÓ, José. *Estudios histórico-artísticos relativos principalmente á Valladolid.* Valladolid-Madrid [1898–1901].
—— *Excursión á Laguna de Duero y el Abrojo* in Sociedad castellana de excursiones. *Boletín.* August 1906. v. 2, p. 443.
—— *Gregorio Fernández, su vida y sus obras* in *Museum.* 1912. v. 2, p. 212–236.
—— *Nuevas noticias de arte extraídas y comentadas de un libro hasta hace poco inédito* in Sociedad castellana de excursiones. *Boletín.* January 1905. v. 2, p. 2–4, 10.

MAYER, August Liebmann. *Zur Entwicklungsgeschichte der Christlichen Plastik in Spanien* in *Zeitschrift für bildende Kunst.* March 1915. v. 26, p. 129–144.

MENDIZABAL, Francisco. *De la vida espiritual*

de Castilla: Arte y santidad in *Blanco y negro*. March 26th, 1922. año 32, no. 1610.

—— *De la vida espiritual de Castilla: El monasterio más rico y más pobre de Valladolid* in *Blanco y negro*. July 3rd, 1921. año 31, no. 1572.

—— *De la vida espiritual de Castilla: Los "santos de pasión" más artísticos de España* in *Blanco y negro*. March 20th, 1921. año 31, no. 1557.

MERLET, J. F. D. *La sculpture sur bois en Espagne* in *L'Art et les artistes*. 1913. v. 17, p. 241–251.

MESONERO ROMANOS, Manuel. *El arte en las iglesias de Madrid* in *La Ilustración española y americana*. January 8th, 1902. año XLVI, p. 13; March 22nd, 1902. año XLVI, p. 170.

MORENO, Anacleto. *Excursión á Avila* in Sociedad castellana de excursiones. *Boletín*. June 1909. v. 4, p. 137.

MUÑOZ, José. *Excursiones por Castilla* in Sociedad española de excursiones. *Boletín*. January 1894. año II, p. 154.

MUÑOZ, Luis. *Vida de la Venerable M. Mariana de S. Iofeph fundadora de la Recoleccion de las Monjas Augustinas, priora del Real Conuento de la Encarnacion.* [Madrid, 1645.] p. 236, 237, 239.

MURGUÍA, Manuel. *Galicia.* Barcelona, 1888. (*España, sus monumentos y artes, su naturaleza é historia.* v. [13]) p. 558–559, 728.

NÚÑEZ, Ramón. *El Cristo del Conjo* in Sociedad castellana de excursiones. *Boletín.* March 1914. v. 6, p. [337]–338.

ORTEGA Y RUBIO, Juan. *Historia de Valladolid.* Valladolid, 1881. 2 v.

ORUETA Y DUARTE, Ricardo de. *Gregorio Hernández.* Madrid, 1920.
—— *La vida y la obra de Pedro de Mena y Medrano.* Madrid, 1914. p. 164–166, 177–180.

PALOMINO DE CASTRO Y VELASCO, Aciscle Antonio. *Las vidas de los pintores y estatuarios eminentes españoles.* Londres, 1742.
—— *and* SANTOS, Francisco de los. *Las ciudades, iglesias y conventos en España, donde ay obras, de los pintores y estatuarios eminentes españoles.* London, 1746. p. 147–148, 173–174.

PARDO BAZÁN, Emilia, *condesa* de. *Por la España pintoresca.* Barcelona [1895?]. p. 117–119.

Passavant, Johann David. *El arte cristiano en España*. Sevilla, 1877. p. [105]–147.

Pinheiro da Veiga, Tomé. *La fastiginia*, tr. by Narciso Alonso Cortés in Sociedad castellana de excursiones. *Boletín*. March 1915. v. 7, p. 56.

Pirala, Antonio. *Provincias vascongadas*. Barcelona, 1885. (*España, sus monumentos y artes, su naturaleza é historia*. v. [1]) p. 132, 297.

Ponz, Antonio. *Viage de España*. Madrid, 1782–94. 18 v.
—— *Viage fuera de España*. Madrid, 1785. v. 1, p. 22, 24–25.

Post, Chandler Rathfon. *A history of European and American sculpture*. Cambridge, 1921. v. 2, p. 73–74.

Quadrado y de la Fuente, José María. *Asturias y León*. Barcelona, 1885. (*España, sus monumentos y artes, su naturaleza é historia*. v. [3]) p. 574.
—— *Salamanca, Avila y Segovia*. Barcelona, 1884. (*España, sus monumentos y artes, su naturaleza é historia*. v. [19]) p. 93, 114, 117.
—— *Valladolid, Palencia y Zamora*. Barcelona, 1885. (*España, sus monumentos y artes, su naturaleza é historia*. v. [24]) p. 62–63.

AND MONOGRAPHS

ROUANET, Léo. *La sculpture sur bois au musée de Valladolid.* (*Extrait de la Revue des Revues, Nº du 1er Janvier 1900*) Paris, 1900. p. 10-14.

SANGRADOR VITORES, Matías. *Historia de la muy noble y leal ciudad de Valladolid.* Valladolid, 1851-54. 2 v.

SERRANO FATIGATI, Enrique. *Escultura en Madrid.* Madrid, 1912. p. 27-31, 101-104.

TORMO Y MONZÓ, Elías. *Cartillas excursionistas "Tormo": Alcalá de Henares* in Sociedad española de excursiones. *Boletín.* June 1917. v. 25, p. 148.
—— *Cartillas excursionistas "Tormo": Avila* in Sociedad española de excursiones. *Boletín.* September 1917. v. 25, p. 214-215.
—— *Cartillas excursionistas "Tormo": El Pardo* in Sociedad española de excursiones. *Boletín.* June 1922. v. 27, p. 150.
—— *Cartillas excursionistas "Tormo": Segovia* in Sociedad española de excursiones. *Boletín.* June 1922. v. 27, p. 133, 135; September 1922. v. 27, p. 206, 208, 210.
—— *La Inmaculada y el arte español.* Madrid, 1915. p. 38-39.
—— *Mis mañanitas valisoletanas: Tras de Becerra, y Goya al paso* in Sociedad castellana de excursiones. *Boletín.* September

1912. v. 5, p. 499–501; October 1912. v. 5, p. [517]–520.

—— Visitando lo no-visitable: Apéndice a la visita a la clausura de la Encarnación in Sociedad española de excursiones. Boletín. September 1917. v. 25, p. 181.

—— Visitando lo no-visitable: La clausura de la Encarnación, de Madrid in Sociedad española de excursiones. Boletín. June 1917. v. 25, p. 126–127.

—— Visitando lo no-visitable: La clausura de las Bernardas del Sacramento in Sociedad española de excursiones. Boletín. June 1921. año XXIX, p. [125]–129.

Valladolid. Museo Provincial. Esculturas notables existentes en el mismo in La Ilustración artística. November 20th, 1916. año XXXV, no. 1821. p. [752–753].

VALLADOLID. Museo provincial de bellas artes. Catálogo de la sección de escultura. [Valladolid] 1916.

VALVERDE Y ALVAREZ, Emilio. Guía de las provincias vascongadas y Navarra. Madrid, 1886. p. 782, 835.

VIÑAZA, Cipriano Muñoz y Manzano, conde de la. Adiciones al diccionario histórico . . . de D. Juan Agustín Ceán Bermúdez. Madrid, 1889–94. 4 v.

INDEX

AND MONOGRAPHS

AND MONOGRAPHS

AND MONOGRAPHS